STORIES OF GREEK GODS, HEROES, AND MEN

A PRIMER OF THE MYTHOLOGY AND HISTORY OF THE GREEKS

SAMUEL BANNISTER HARDING

CAROLINE HIRST HARDING

FV EDITIONS

CONTENTS

STORIES OF THE HEROES

STORIES FROM GREEK HISTORY

PREFACE

A justification of such a book as this is happily no longer necessary. The value of the old Greek stories as material of the cultivation of the child's imagination and the development of the ethical perceptions has long been admitted; and since the report of the conference on History to the Committee of Ten appointed by the National Education Association, some five years ago, the necessity of basing the formal study of History on some sort of elementary studies in biography and mythology has steadily become more and more generally recognized.

These are the ends which this little book is intended to sub serve; and that it will sub serve them, if intelligently used, is the firm conviction of its authors. The book is not altogether an untried one. Both of the authors have had practical experience in the use of such stories in primary classes; and many of the chapters here presented have been used by

one of the authors as reading materials and as the
basis for composition writing in the third and fourth
year of work of the Indianapolis public schools. In
giving them to the public, therefore, the authors
only hope that the stories may prove as satisfactory
in a more extended use as they have been in the lim-
ited field in which they have been tried.

In preparing the stories, the authors have tried
to keep constantly in touch with the Greek literature
from which the tales are ultimately derived. When
more than one version of a story exists, choice has
been made of that one which seems best adapted to
further the objects above indicated. The Greek
names have been retained in accordance with what
is now recognized as the only scholarly usage.

BLOOMINGTON, INDIANA.
October, 1897.

STORIES OF THE GODS

1

THE GREEKS

The Acropolis at Athens.

F ar, far away from our own country, across wide seas and many strange lands, is a beautiful country called Greece. There the sky is bluer than our own; the winters are short and mild, and the summers long and pleasant. In whatever direction you look, in that land, you may see the top of some tall mountain reaching up toward the sky Between the mountains lie beautiful deep valleys, and small sunny plains, while almost all around the land stretches a bright blue sea.

The people who live in that country are called Greeks, and are not very different now from ourselves. But many centuries ago this was not true. In those long-ago days, there were no newspapers, no railroads, no telegraph lines, such as we are used to now. The people were obliged to live very simply then, and did not have a great many things that we think we could not possibly do without.

But although the old Greeks did not know anything of electric lights and steam engines, and ate the plainest food, and wore the simplest of woolen clothing, they were not at all a rude or savage people. In their cities were fine buildings, and pictures, and statues so beautiful that we can never hope to make better ones. And they had lovely thoughts and fancies, too, for all the world about them.

When they saw the sun rise, they thought that it was a great being called a god, who came up out of the sea in the east, and then journeyed across the ky toward the west. When they saw the grass and wers springing up out of the dark cold earth, they fancied that there must be another god who made them grow. They imagined that the lightning was the weapon of a mighty god, who ruled the earth and sky. And so they explained everything about them, by thinking that it was caused by some being much greater than themselves. Sometimes they even imagined that they could see their gods in the clouds or in the waves of the sea, and sometimes they thought that they heard them speaking in the rustling leaves of the forest.

The Greeks believed that the whole world was divided among three great gods, who were brothers The first and greatest of these was the god of the heaven and earth. The second was the god of the ocean, the rivers, and the brooks. The third was the god of the under-world, or the dark space beneath the surface of the ground. But besides these, there were many other gods, most of whom were the children of these three or related to them in some way.

The gods were always thought of as larger than men and more beautiful in face and figure They remained always the same, never growing older or dying, as men do. They were not always good, but would often quarrel among themselves, and sometimes do very cruel things. Indeed, they were very much like the men and women who imagined them, except that they could do wonderful things which would have been impossible for the people of the earth.

Besides the greater gods, the Greeks believed that less powerful spirits were all about them. They thought that the trees had guardian spirits who cared for them. Lovely maidens, called Nymphs, were supposed to live in the springs and brooks, and even in the bright waves of the sea. There were spirits, too, who lived in the woods, and wandered among the trees day and night; and still others who made their homes upon the mountain sides.

The Greeks loved their gods, but feared them a little also. They tried to gain their good-will by building beautiful marble temples in their honor, and by offering wine and meat and precious things to them. They never grew tired of thinking and talking about their gods. So they made up many beautiful stories about them, which they told and re-told, and which their children and grandchildren repeated after them for many hundreds of years.

2

ZEUS, THE KING OF THE GODS

Фиг. 11.

In the northern part of Greece there was a very high mountain called Mount Olympus; so high that during almost all the year its top was covered with snow, and often, too, it was wrapped in clouds. Its sides were very steep, and covered with thick forests of oak and beech trees.

The Greeks thought that the palaces of their gods were above the top of this mountain, far out of the reach of men, and hidden from their sight by the clouds. Here they thought that the gods met together in a grand council hall, and held great feasts, at which they talked over the affairs of the whole world.

Zeus, who ruled over the land and the air, was the king of the gods, and was the greatest and strongest among them. The strength of all the other gods put together could not overcome him. It was he who caused the clouds to form, and who sent the rain to refresh the thirsty earth. His great weapon was the thunderbolt, which he carried in his right hand. But the thunderbolt was seldom used, for the frown and angry nod of Zeus were enough to shake the palaces of the gods themselves.

Although Zeus was so powerful, he was also king and generous to those who pleased him. The people who lived upon the earth loved as well as feared him, and called him father. He was the most just of all the gods. Once when there was a great war between the Greeks and another people, all the other gods took sides, and tried to help those whom they favored all they could. But Zeus did not. He tried to be just, and at last he gave the victory to the side which he thought deserved to have it.

The oak was thought to be sacred to Zeus because it was the strongest and grandest of all the trees. In one part of Greece there was a forest of these, which was called the forest of Dodona. It was so thick and that the sunbeams scarcely found their way through the leaves to the moss upon the ground. Here the wind made strange low sounds among the knotted branches, and people soon began to think that this was their great god Zeus speaking to men through the leaves of his favorite tree So they set this forest apart as sacred to him; and only his servants, who were called priests, were allowed to live in it. People came to this place from all parts of Greece to ask the advice of the god; and the priests would consult with him, and hear his answers in the murmuring of the wind among the branches.

The Greeks also built beautiful temples for their gods, as we build churches. To these temples they brought rich gifts of gold and silver and other precious things, to show how thankful they were for the help which the gods gave them. In each temple there was a great block of marble called the altar, and on this a small fire was often kept burning by the priests. If anyone wished to get the help of one of the gods, he would bring a dove, or a goat, or an ox to the temple, so that the priests might kill it, and burn part of its flesh as an offering. For they thought that the smell of the burning flesh pleased the gods.

Since Zeus was the greatest of the gods, many of the most beautiful temples in Greece were built in his honor. A part of one of these temples to Zeus is still standing, and you can see it if you ever go to Greece. It was made of the finest white marble, and was surrounded on all sides by rows of tall columns beautifully carved

In another temple there was a great statue of Zeus, made of ivory and gold. It was over sixty feet high, and showed the god seated on a great throne which was covered with carving The robe of the god was of solid gold. But it was the face of the statue which the Greeks though was most wonderful. It was so grand and beautiful that they said: "Either the sculptor must have gone up into heaven and seen Zeus upon his throne, or the god must have come down to earth and shown his face to the artist."

Besides building temples for their gods, the Greeks held great festivals in their honor also. The greatest of these festivals was the one which was held in honor of Zeus at a place called Olympia. Every four years messengers would go about from town to town to give notice of it. Then all wars would cease, and people from all over Greece would come to Olympia to worship the god. There they would find the swiftest runners racing for a wreath of olive leaves as a prize. There they would also find chariot races and wrestling matches and other games. The Greeks believed that Zeus and the other gods loved to see men using their strength and skill to do them honor at their festivals. So for months and months beforehand men practiced for these games; and the one who gained the victory in them was looked upon as ever after the favorite of gods and men.

3

POSEIDON, THE GOD OF THE SEA.

Poseidon was the brother of Zeus, and just as Zeus ruled over the land and the sky, Poseidon ruled over the rivers and the seas. He was always represented as carrying a trident, or fish-spear with three points. When he struck the sea with this, fierce storms would arise; then with a word he could quiet the dashing waves, and make the surface of the water as smooth as that of a pond.

The palace of Poseidon was said to be at the bottom of the sea. It was made of shells and coral, fastened together with gold and silver. The floors were of pearl, and were ornamented with all kids of precious stones. Around the palace were great gardens filled with beautiful sea-plants and vines. The flowers were of the softest and most delicate tints, and were far more beautiful than those growing in the light of the sun. The leaves were not of the deep green which we see on land, but of a most lovely sea-green color. If you should ever go to the sea-coast, and look down through the water, perhaps you also might see the gardens of Poseidon lying among the rocks at the bottom of the sea.

Poseidon rode over the surface of the sea in a chariot made of a huge sea-shell, which was drawn by great sea-horses with golden hoofs and manes. At the approach of the god, the waves would grow quiet, and strange fishes and huge sea-serpents and sea-lions would come to the surface to play about his chariot. Wonderful creatures called Tritons went before and beside his chariot, blowing upon shells as trumpets These Tritons had green hair and eyes; their bodies were like those of men, but instead of legs they had tails like fishes.

Nymphs also swam along by the sea-god's chariot. Some of these were like the Tritons, half human and half fish. Others were like lovely maidens, with fair faces and hair. Some lived so much in the depths of the sea that their soft blue eyes could not bear the light of day. So they never left the water except in the evening, when they would find some quiet place upon the shore, and dance to the music which they made upon delicate sea-shells.

Poseidon once had a quarrel with one of the goddesses over a piece of land which each one wished to own, and at last they asked the other gods to settle the dispute for them. So at a meeting on Mount Olympus the gods decided that the one who should make the most useful gift to the people should have the land.

When the trial came, Poseidon thought that a spring of water would be an excellent gift He struck a great blow with his trident upon a rocky hill that stood in that land, and a stream of water gushed forth. But Poseidon had lived so much in the sea that he had forgotten that men could drink only fresh water. The spring which he had made was as salt as salt could be, and it was of no use to the people at all. Then the goddess, in her turn, caused an olive-tree to spring up out of the ground. When the gods saw how much use men could make of its fruit and oil, they decided that the goddess had won. So Poseidon did not get the land; but ever afterward the people showed the salt spring and the olive-tree upon the hill-top as a proof that the trial had taken place.

Poseidon was worshiped most by the people who lived by the shore of the sea. Every city along the coast had a temple to Poseidon, where people came to pray to him for fair weather and happy voyages for themselves and for their friends.

4

HADES, THE KING OF THE DEAD.

Hades, the god of the under-world, was also a brother of Zeus; but the Greeks did not think of him as being bright and beautiful like the other gods. They believed, indeed, that he helped make the seeds sprout and push their leaves above the surface of the earth, and that he gave men the gold and silver which they dug out of their mines. But more often they thought of him as the god of the gloomy world of the dead; so they imagined that he was dark and stern in appearance, and they feared him more than they did the other gods.

The Greeks thought that when any one died, his soul or shade went at once to the kingdom of Hades. The way to this under-world lay through a cave which was in the midst of a dark and gloomy forest, by the side of a still lake. When they had passed down through this cavern, the shades came to a broad, swift stream of black water. There they found a bent old man named Charon, whose duty it was to take the shades across the stream in a small, leaky boat. But only those spirits could cross whose bodies had been properly burned or buried in the world above; and those whose funerals had not been properly attended to were compelled to wander for a hundred years upon the river-bank before Charon would take them across.

When the shades had crossed the river, they came upon a terrible creature, which guarded the path so that no one who had once passed into the kingdom of the dead could ever come out again. This was the great dog Cerberus, who had three heads, and who barked so fiercely that he could be heard through all the lower world.

Beyond him the shades entered the judgment room, where they were judged for what they had done on earth. If they had lived good lives, they were allowed to enter the fields of the blessed, where flowers of gold bloomed in beautiful meadows; and there they walked and talked with other shades, who had led good lives in the world above. But the Greeks thought that even these spirits were always longing to see the light of day again, for they believed that no life was so happy as that which they lived on the face of the earth.

The shades who had lived bad lives in the world above were dreadfully punished in the world of the dead. There was once a king named Sisyphus, who had been cruel and wicked all his life. When he died, and his shade went down to the under-world, the judge told him that his punishment would be to roll a great stone up a steep hill and down the other side. At first Sisyphus thought that this would be an easy thing to do. But when he had got the stone almost to the top, and it seemed that one more push would send it over and end his task, it suddenly slipped from his hands, and rolled to the foot of the hill again. So it happened every time; and the Greeks believed that Sisyphus would have to keep working in this way as long as the world lasted, and that his task would never be done.

There was once another king, named Tantalus, who was wealthy and fortunate upon earth, and had been loved by the gods of heaven. Zeus had even invited him to sit at his table once, and had told him the secrets of the gods. But Tantalus had not proved worthy of all this honor. He had not been able to keep the secrets that had been trusted to him, but had told them to all the world. So when his shade came before the judge of the dead, he, too, was given a dreadful punishment. He was chained in the midst of a sparkling little lake where the water came up almost to his lips. He was always burning with thirst; but whenever he stooped to drink from the lake, the water sank into the ground before him. He was always hungry, and branches loaded with delicious fruits hung just over him. But whenever he raised his hand to gather them, the breeze swung them just out of his reach. In this way the Greeks thought that Tantalus was to be punished forever because he had told the secrets of the gods.

5

HERA, THE QUEEN OF THE GODS

The wife of Zeus was the tall and beautiful goddess Hera. As Zeus was the king of all the gods, so she was their queen. She sat beside him in the council-hall of the gods, on a throne only a little less splendid than his own. She was the greatest of all the goddesses, and was extremely proud of her own strength and beauty.

Hera chose the peacock for her favorite bird, because its plumage was so beautiful. The goddess Iris was her servant and messenger, and flew swiftly through the air upon her errands. The rainbow, which seemed to join heaven and earth with its beautiful arch, was thought to be the road by which Iris traveled.

Here was not only proud of her own beauty, but she was also very jealous of the beauty of any one else. She would even punish women that she thought were too beautiful, as if they had done something very wrong; she often did this by changing them into animals or birds. There was one woman whom Hera changed into the form of a savage bear, and turned out to wander in the forest because she hated her beautiful face. The poor creature was terribly frightened among the fierce animals of the woods; for although she herself now had the form of a beast, her soul was still human. At last Zeus, who was kinder of heart than Hera, took pity upon her. He lifted her far above the earth, and placed her among the stars of heaven; and so, ever after that, the Greeks called one group of stars the Great Bear.

There was once a wood-nymph named Echo, who deceived Hera, and so made her very angry Echo was a merry, beautiful girl, whose tongue was always going, and who was never satisfied unless she could have the last word. As a punishment for her deception, Hera took away her voice, leaving her only the power to repeat the last word that should be spoken to her. Echo now no longer cared to join her companions in their merry games, and so wandered through the forests all alone. But she longed to talk, and would often hide in the woods, and repeat the words of hunters and others who passed that way.

At last she learned to take delight in puzzling and mocking the people who listened to her.

"Who are you?" they would shout at her.

"You," would come her answer.

"Then, who am I?" they would ask, still more puzzled.

"I," Echo would answer in her sweet, teasing manner.

One day Echo met in the woods a young man named Narcissus, and loved him. But he was very unkind, and would take no notice of her except to tease her for the loss of her voice. She became very unhappy, and began to waste away from grief, until at last there was nothing left of her but her beautiful mocking voice.

When the gods found what had happened to the lovely Echo they were very angry. To punish Narcissus for his unkindness, they changed him from a strong young man to a weak, delicate flower, which is now always called by his name.

6

APOLLO, THE GOD OF LIGHT

Apollo was the son of Zeus, and was one of the greatest of the gods of Mount Olympus. He was often called the sung-god, because the Greeks thought that he brought the sun's light and warmth to men. As these are so necessary to every living thing, they thought that Apollo was also the god of health and manly beauty. So he was always represented by the Greeks in their pictures and statues as a strong and beautiful young man.

Apollo was very fond of music, and was in the habit of playing upon the lyre at the feasts of the gods, to the great delight of all who heard him. He was very proud of his skill, and would often have contests with the other gods, and sometimes even with men.

At one of these contests, a king named Midas was present. But instead of deciding , as was usual, that Apollo was much the more skillful player, he was better pleased with another. Apollo became very angry at this, and to show his opinion of Midas he changed his ears into those of a donkey.

It was then the turn of Midas to be vexed. He wore a cap which hid his large, ugly ears; and he allowed no one to learn what had happened to him except the man who cut his hair. Midas made this man promise that he would tell no one of his misfortune But the man longed so to tell that at last he could stand it no longer. He went to the edge of a stream, dug a hole in the earth, and whispered into it the secret Then he filled up the hole, and went away satisfied. But up from that spot sprang a bunch of reeds, which immediately began to whisper on every breeze, "King Midas has donkey's ears; King Midas has donkey's ears." And so the story was soon known to the whole world.

The Greeks thought that Apollo caused sudden death among men by shooting swift arrows which never failed of their aim. In this way he punished the wicked, and gave welcome death to the good who were suffering and wished to die.

There was once a great queen named Niobe, who had six sons and six daughters. She was proud of her beauty, and proud of her wealth and power, but proudest of all of her twelve beautiful children. She thought that they were so beautiful, and she loved them so much, that she even dared to boast that she was greater than the mother of Apollo, who had but two children.

This made the goddess very angry, and she begged her son to punish the queen for her wicked pride. Apollo, with his bow and arrows at his side, floated down to the earth hid in a cloud. There he saw the sons of Niobe playing games among the other boys of the city. Quickly he pierced one after another of them with his arrows, and soon the six lay dead upon the ground. The frightened people took up the dead boys gently, and carried them home to their mother. She was broken-hearted, but cried,—

"The gods have indeed punished me, but they have left me my beautiful daughters"

She had scarcely spoken when one after another her daughters fell dead at her feet. Niobe clasped the youngest in her arms to save her from the deadly arrows. When this one, too, was killed, the queen could bear no more. Her great grief turned her to stone, and the people thought that for many years her stone figure stood there with tears flowing constantly from its sad eyes.

One of the most famous temples in Greece was built to Apollo at a place called Delphi. Here there was always a priestess, whose duty it was to tell the people who came there the answers which the god gave to their questions. She would place herself on a seat over a crack in the earth out of which arose a thin stream of gases. By breathing this she was made light-headed for the moment, and then she was supposed to be able to tell the answer which Apollo gave.

These answers were almost always in poetry; and though they were very wise sayings, it was sometimes hard to tell just what the god meant by them. Once a great king wished to begin a war, and asked the advice of Apollo about it at Delphi. The priestess answered, that if he went to war he would destroy a great nation. The king thought that this must mean that he would conquer his enemies, and so he began the war. But, alas, he was conquered himself, and found that it was his own nation which was to be destroyed.

Although these oracles, as they were called, were so hard to understand, the Greeks thought a great deal of them; and they would never begin anything important without first asking the advice of Apollo.

7

____

ARTEMIS, THE HUNTRESS-GODDESS

Artemis was the twin sister of Apollo, and like him she was very skillful with the bow and arrow. When very young, she went to her father, Zeus, and begged him to allow her to live a free and happy life upon the beautiful mountains. Zeus granted her wish, and so she became the great huntress-goddess of the fields and forests.

As Apollo was the god of the sun and the bright daylight, so Artemis was the goddess of the moon. She loved to hunt by moonlight; and when the Greeks made statues of her, they sometimes represented her with a torch held high in one hand and a bow in the other. Artemis always had a band of maidens with her, who ran beside her, and took care of her dogs, and carried her arrows. She could run so swiftly that she could overtake the fleetest deer in the hunt. She and her maidens would dash through the forests with cries and merry laughter, and then when the hunt was over they would bathe in the pure mountain streams.

Artemis loved the woods and mountains so dearly that she rarely left them for the cities of men. But she was very selfish in her love of them, and did not wish to be disturbed in her enjoyment. There was once a young man named Actaeon, who was a great hunter, and who often wandered through the forests alone with his dogs. One day he came upon the goddess Artemis, playing with her maidens upon the banks of a stream. Instead of going away at once, as he should have done, he stood quite still and watched them. This made Artemis so angry that she changed him into a deer, and his own dogs then turned upon him, and tore him to pieces.

Artemis loved all the animals of the forest, but her favorite was the deer. Once a great king of the Greeks killed a doe of which Artemis was very fond. This king was just starting out upon a great war, and he had many vessels in the harbor all ready to sail. But day after day passed, and the wind blew constantly from the wrong direction, and the vessels could not put out to sea. The Greeks grew impatient, and asked the priest why it was that the gods gave them no fair breeze.

Then the priest consulted the gods, and told the people that Artemis was angry because the king had killed her doe, and that she would not let the right winds blow until the king gave up his young daughter to be sacrificed upon the altar of the goddess At first the king refused to do this, for he loved his daughter greatly; but at last he had to consent.

Then the beautiful girl was led to the altar, and the priest raised his long knife to strike. But before it fell upon her breast, a cloud dropped over her, and hid her from sight. When it floated away the girl was nowhere to be seen; only a white doe remained in her place, and this the priest sacrificed in her stead.

The goddess had taken pity upon the maiden, and carried her in the midst of that thick cloud far away to a distant country. There she served for a long time as priestess in one of the temples to Artemis. But at last, after many years, her brother found her, and she was allowed to come back to her own country and friends once more.

8

ATHENA, THE GODDESS OF WISDOM.

Athena was one of the most powerful of the goddesses. She was called the daughter of Zeus; but the Greeks believed that she had sprung full grown from his head, wearing her helmet and armor. She was more warlike than the other goddesses, and was almost always successful in her battles.

Athena was the goddess of wisdom and learning. The owl was her favorite bird, because of its wise and solemn look, and it is often represented with Athena in the images which the Greeks made of her.

While Artemis loved most the woods and mountains, Athena like the cities better. There she watched over the work and occupations of men, and helped them to find out better ways of doing things. For them she invented the plow and the rake; and she taught men to yoke oxen to the plow that they might till the soil better and more easily. She also made the first bridle, and showed men how to tame horses with it, and make them work for them. She invented the chariot, and the flute, and the trumpet; and she taught men how to count and use numbers. Besides all this, Athena was the goddess of spinning and weaving; and she herself could weave the most beautiful cloths of many colors and of the most marvelous patterns.

There was once a girl named Arachne, who was a skillful weaver, and who was also very proud of her skill. Indeed, she was so proud that once she boasted that she could weave as well as the goddess Athena herself. The goddess heard this boast, and came to Arachne in the form of an old woman. She advised the girl to take back her words, but Arachne refused. Then the bent old woman changed suddenly into the goddess Athena. Arachne was startled and surprised, but in an instant she was ready for the test of skill which the goddess demanded. The two stood at looms side by side, and wove cloth covered with the most wonderful pictures. When the goddess discovered that she could find no fault with Arachne's work, she became terribly angry. She struck Arachne, and tore the cloth on her loom. Arachne was so frightened by the anger of the goddess that she tried to kill herself. Athena then became sorry for the girl, and saved her life by changing her into a spider. So Arachne lives to this day, and still weaves the most wonderful of all webs upon our walls and ceilings, and upon the grasses by the roadside.

It was not often, though, that Athena was so spiteful as you must think her from the story of Arachne. Usually she was kind and generous; and nothing pleased her better than to help brave, honest men, especially if they were skillful and clever.

The Greeks loved to tell the story of one such man whom Athena helped. His name was Odysseus, and in a great war of the Greeks he had proved himself to be one of the bravest and most cunning of all their chiefs. But in some way he had displeased the god Poseidon so much that when the war was over, and all the other Greeks sailed away in safety, Poseidon would not permit him to reach his far-off home. So for ten years Odysseus was kept far from his wife and child. He was blown about by storms, his ship was wrecked, and he had to meet and overcome giants and all sorts of monsters. Indeed, he had to make a trip down into the dark world of the dead before he could find out how he might manage to get back to his home again. But through it all, Athena was his friend. She watched over him, and encouraged him, and in each difficulty she taught him some trick by which he could escape. At last, after he had suffered much, and had even lost all of the men who had started with him, she brought him safely home again, in spite of all that Poseidon could do to prevent it.

9

———

HEPHAESTUS, THE SMITH-GOD

Hephaestus, the god of fire and metal-working, was the son of Zeus and Hera. While he was a child, he lived with the sea-nymphs in an ocean cavern. From his very babyhood he could make all kinds of useful and beautiful things, and it was his constant delight to be planning some marvelous invention. When he was grown, he took his place on Mount Olympus with the other gods, and was always busy making things either for himself or for them. Among other wonderful things, he made magic shoes that could tread water or air as easily as earth; caps which made the persons who wore them invisible; and gold and silver dishes that would carry themselves away from the table, without the aid of servants.

Hephaestus had his forge and workshop in his own palace on Mount Olympus. He trained many servants to aid him in his work, and planned twenty great bellows for his forge, which would blow his fire into a fierce heat at a word from him. He had other workshops upon the earth; and wherever there was a volcano with smoke and fire coming from its summit, the people said that there Hephaestus was busy with his giant helpers making wonderful things for the gods.

As you have learned, the gods and goddesses were not always good and kind. One day Hera made her husband angry; and to punish her, Zeus fastened her hands and feet together, and hung her in the air midway between heaven and earth. This was a very cruel way to treat the beautiful and stately Hera, and all the gods pitied her. Hephaestus was so sorry for his mother that he tried to set her free. This made Zeus still more angry, and he struck him so heavily in his rage that poor Hephaestus was thrown headlong from the sky.

Down, down he fell for a whole day, and struck the earth at last upon a beautiful island The fall did not kill him, for he was one of the immortal gods, and could not die; but he fell with such force that he was lame ever afterwards.

Zeus was too deeply angry to allow Hephaestus to return at once to his home among the gods, so he was forced to remain upon his island. After he had recovered from his fall he used to wander about his new home, seeking something with which to busy himself. He found great quantities of gold and silver; but he had no furnace, and so could do nothing with them. But one day he heard a strange rumbling in the earth, and following the sound he came upon a newly formed volcano.

"Here is my furnace," he exclaimed, and immediately began to cut a hole in the mountain to get at the fire. There he set up his workshop, and brought to it some of the gold and silver which he had found. From this he made many wonderful and beautiful things. Among them he made some new thunderbolts, and sent them as a gift to Zeus. In return for these, Zeus recalled him to Mount Olympus.

Hephaestus must have looked very strange in the meetings of the gods after this; for he was ugly and crippled from his fall, while the others were straight and beautiful. But he was the kindest and best-natured of them all, and often served as peacemaker among them. Once while he was trying to settle a quarrel in the assembly of the gods, he took the place of the cup-bearer, and handed about the cup of wine from which they used to drink. But he was so awkward about it that the other gods burst into a shout of laughter as he went limping about. Hephaestus did not care, however; for he had succeeded in stopping the quarrel, and that was what he had wished to do.

10

APHRODITE, THE GODDESS OF BEAUTY

The most beautiful of all the goddesses was Aphrodite, the goddess of love and beauty. She was often called the "sea-born" goddess, because she was formed one evening from the foam of the sea, where its waves beat upon a rocky shore. Her eyes were as blue as the summer sky overhead, her skin as fair as the white sea-foam from which she came, and her hair as golden as the yellow rays of the setting sun. When she stepped from the water upon the beach, flowers sprang up under her feet; and when she was led into the assembly of the gods, every one admired and loved her.

Zeus, in order to make up for his cruelty to Hephaestus, gave him this beautiful goddess for his wife. The gods prepared for them the grandest wedding possible. All the gods and goddesses were there, bringing with them magnificent gifts for the bride.

But the most wonderful of all were the presents given her by Hephaestus himself.

He built many palaces for her, the most marvelous of which was on the island of Cyprus. In the middle of this island was a large blue lake, in which there was another island Upon this Hephaestus built a palace of white marble, with towers and ornaments of gold and silver. It was then filled with wonderful things which the skillful god made to please his wife. Among these were servants of solid gold, that would obey the wishes of Aphrodite without word or sound. There were also golden harps, which made sweet music all day long, without any one playing upon them; and golden birds, which sang the sweetest of songs.

All birds were great favorites of Aphrodite, and they loved her as much as she loved them They taught her their bird language, so that she talked with them as though they had been persons. Of all them, however, she liked the doves and swans the best. Doves fluttered around her head and alighted, on her arms and shoulders, wherever she went; and swans drew her back and forth in a beautiful boat across the waters between her palace and the shore of the lake.

Aphrodite was the kindest and gentlest of the goddesses. The Greeks did not pray to her for power, as they did to Zeus, or for learning and wisdom, as they did to Athena. Instead, they prayed to her to make the persons they cared for love them in return

Once a sculptor, named Pygmalion, tried to

make a statue that should be more lovely than the loveliest woman. He chose the finest ivory, and for months and months he worked patiently at his task. As it began to take the form of a beautiful maiden under his skillful chisel, he became so interested in his work that he scarcely took time to eat or sleep. At last the work was finished, and everybody said that the statue was more beautiful than any woman that had ever lived.

But Pygmalion was not satisfied. All day long he would sit in front of his statue and look at it. He came to love it so much at last, that he wished over and over again that it were a real woman, so that t might talk to him, and love him in return. He longed for this in secret until at last he grew bold enough tot ask the gods for help. Then he went to the temple of Aphrodite, and there before the altar he prayed to the goddess to change his statue into a real woman. As he finished his prayer, he saw the altar-fire flame up three times, and he knew that the goddess had heard him. He hastened home, and there he found that his statue of ivory had indeed been turned into a woman of flesh and blood; and all his life long he blessed the goddess Aphrodite for granting his wish.

11

───────

HERMES, THE MESSENGER OF THE GODS

The Greeks did not always think of their gods as grown-up persons. Sometimes they told stories of their youth and even of their babyhood. According to these stories the god Hermes, who was the son of Zeus, must have been a very wonderful child. They said that when he was but a day old his nurses left him asleep, as they supposed, in his cradle. But the moment that their backs were turned, he climbed out and ran away.

For quite a while he wandered about over the fields and hills, until, by and by, he came upon a herd of cattle that belonged to his elder brother Apollo. These he drove off, and hid in a cave in the mountains. Then, as he thought that by this time his nurses would be expecting him to wake up, he started for home. On the way he came upon a tortoise-shell in the road, and from this he made a harp or lyre by stretching strings tightly across it. He amused himself by playing upon this until he reached home, where he crept back into his cradle again.

Apollo soon discovered the loss of his fine cattle, and was told by an old man that the baby Hermes had driven them away. He went to the mother of Hermes in great anger, and told her that her baby had stolen his cattle. She was astonished, of course, that any one should say such a thing of a baby only a day old, and showed Apollo the child lying in his cradle, fast asleep as it seemed. But Apollo was not deceived by the child's innocent look. He insisted upon taking him to Mount Olympus; and there before his father Zeus, and the other gods, he accused Hermes of having stolen the herd of oxen.

At first Hermes denied that he had done anything of the kind; and he talked so fast and so well, in defending himself, that all the gods were amused and delighted. Zeus, however, was the most pleased of all; for he was proud of a son who could do such wonderful things while he was so young. But for all his cleverness, Hermes at last had to confess that he had driven the cattle off, and had to go with Apollo, and show him where he had hidden them.

All this time Hermes had with him the lyre which he had made from the tortoise-shell, and as they went along he began to play upon this for Apollo. As you know, Apollo was very fond of music, so he was greatly delighted with this new instrument which Hermes had invented. When Hermes saw how pleased Apollo was he gave him the lyre Apollo was so charmed with the gift, that he quite forgave Hermes for the trick he played him, and, indeed, gave him the whole herd of cattle for his own, in return for the little lyre.

As soon as he was grown, Hermes was made the messenger, or herald, of the gods. He was chosen for this position because he had shown so early that he was a good talkers, and so would be able to deliver the messages well. In order that he might be able to do his errands quickly, he wore a pair of winged sandals on his feet, which carried him through the air as swiftly as a flash of lightning.

He was especially the herald of Zeus. The Greeks though that their dreams came from Zeus himself, and that is was Hermes who brought them, flying swiftly downward through the darkness of the night. But besides this, Hermes served as messenger for all the gods, even for Hades in the under-world. When people died, the Greeks thought that it was Hermes who guided their shades to their dark home underneath the ground

Because he traveled so much himself, Hermes was supposed to take care of all men who traveled upon the earth. In those days it was a far more dangerous thing to make a journey than it is now. Then men had to walk nearly always when they wished to go from one place to another. The roads were bad, and often were only narrow paths that one could scarcely follow. In some places, too, there were robbers who would lie in wait for travelers coming along that way. So, before starting, travelers would offer sacrifices to Hermes, and pray to him to protect them, and grant them a safe journey. All along the roads, were posts of wood, upon which the head of Hermes was carved. These usually stood at the meeting of two roads, and were guideposts, to tell the travelers which way to take.

12

———

ARES, THE GOD OF WAR

res was the god of war and battle, and cared for almost nothing else. The Greeks believed that the other gods protected them, or helped them in useful ways, and so they loved them. But the only help they could ever expect to get from Ares was that which he might give them when they were at war, and even then he might be on the other side. So, instead of loving him as they did Zeus and Apollo and Athena, they dreaded him, and called him "bloody Ares," and "raging Ares," because of his fierce temper. And although they worshiped him, they did not care to build quite so many temples in his honor as they did for the other gods.

Nothing pleased Ares better than a battle between two great armies. He liked to see the chiefs driving furiously toward each other in their war chariots, with helmets on their heads, and shields on their arms. He liked to see them throw their spears, and shoot their arrows, and strike with their swords at one another. The roar and confusion of the battlefield were delightful to him, and the more men that were killed the better he liked it. Indeed, Ares was so fond of battle that he would often come down from heaven, and take part himself in the fights of men. Then the strongest and bravest of warriors had to give way before him. But although the god was so fond of war, he was not so successful in it as the goddess Athena She used wisdom and cunning to help her in her battles; while Ares never stopped to think, but plunged ahead.

Once during a great war, Ares was fighting against the Greeks, and driving them all before him. When Athena saw this, she went to their aid; for she thought that they had been right in the quarrel which had begun the war, and she did not wish to see them defeated. When Ares saw her upon the Greek side in all her armor, he rushed toward her, and threw his terrible spear against her breast. Athena caught the spear point on her shield, and turned it aside. Then she seized a great rock, and hurled it at Ares. Her aim was so sure that it struck him squarely, and knocked him flat upon his back. He was such an enormous fellow that it was said that his body covered seven acres as he lay there on the ground. Ares was so injured by the blow, that he gave up the fight, and fled to Mount Olympus. Then the Greeks, with the help of Athena, won the victory.

The Greeks loved to tell another story about the way in which Ares was once made prisoner. Long,

long ago, they said, two boys were born who were named Otus and Ephialtes. At first they were small and weak, but they grew so rapidly that they soon astonished all men by their size and beauty. When they were yet only nine years old, they had become giants many feet tall, and they were as brave as they were huge. Now, these giants were farmers, and loved to live in peace, and care for their growing grain. But Ares stirred up such constant war among men that their crops were often destroyed, and their fields laid bare.

At last Otus and Ephialtes became very angry at this, and determined to see what they could do to stop it. They were so strong and brave that they had no fear of Ares at all; so they planned and planned, and one day succeeded in taking the war-god prisoner Then, in order to keep him securely, they put him in a great bronze vase. After this, for thirteen months, there were no wars, and their grain fields were undisturbed In spite of all he could do, Ares could not get out; and indeed, he might have had to stay there forever if Hermes had not discovered what had become of him, and set him free.

13

DEMETER, THE EARTH-GODDESS

Demeter was the sister of Zeus, and was the goddess who watched over the fertile earth and the plants that grew out of it. She taught men how to sow grain, and how to cultivate it; so the Greeks worshiped her as the goddess of agriculture. When they made pictures or statues of her, they represented her as carrying bunches of grain and poppies in her hands.

Demeter had a beautiful young daughter named Persephone, whom she loved very much, and who helped her in caring for the grain that men planted. When the seed was dropped into the ground, Persephone watched over it, and guarded it until the tiny green leaves pushed out of the dark earth. Then Demeter cared for it until the plant was grown and the grain was ripened.

One day the young goddess was playing with a

number of nymphs in a beautiful meadow. Beds of violets and crocuses and other flowers were growing there, and Persephone was gathering some of the prettiest of the blossoms. Suddenly a great opening appeared in the earth at her feet, and out of this a chariot came rushing. The poor girl was seized, and placed in it, and carried swiftly away in spite of her cries.

When Demeter found that Persephone had been stolen from her, she was almost wild with grief. She lighted a torch, and mounted her chariot drawn by winged snakes, and for nine days and nine nights she searched for her daughter without stopping to eat or to drink. On the tenth day the Sun told her that Zeus had given Persephone to Hades to be his queen, and that he had taken her to the under-world. Then Demeter was very angry. She went far away from the homes of the gods, and hid herself on earth, where she mourned a long time for her daughter.

One day the goddess was sitting by the side of a well, dressed all in black, and looking like some wrinkled old woman, when four young girls came to the well to draw water They were sorry for the old woman, because she seemed so sad and lonely; and they took her home with them to their mother. They did not know, of course, that this old woman was a goddess; but they were all very kind to her, and the mother kept her to nurse her baby son. The little boy reminded the goddess so much of her own child that she grew very fond of him. She wished to make him immortal like the gods, so that he might never grow old or die; and at night, when every one else was asleep, she would lay the child in the fire to burn away the mortal part. But one night the baby's mother was watching, and screamed aloud when she saw him in the flames. That broke the charm. But though Demeter could not make the boy immortal after that, she did cause him to grow up to be a great and good man.

While Demeter was thus searching for her daughter, there was no one to look after the grain. The seed which was planted in the ground failed to come up; and though men plowed and plowed, nothing would grow. By and by Zeus saw that unless the gods could get Demeter to care for the grain again, the race of men would all die. So he sent the gods one after another to beg her to come back to Mount Olympus. But she refused to do so unless they would give her back her daughter.

Then Zeus sent Hermes down into the under-world to get Persephone. But when he had returned with her they found that she had eaten part of a pomegranate, or love-apple, while she was with Hades; and so she could only be given back to her mother for part of each year.

After that, for two-thirds of the year Persephone was allowed to live with her mother in the light and air of the upper world, but the remainder of the time she was obliged to stay with Hades as queen of the under-world. The Greeks thought that when the bright springtime came it was Persephone returning

to her mother, and making all the earth glad by her
presence. But when the winter winds blew, and the
plants and flowers died, then, they said, she had returned underground, and the earth was left dark
and dreary.

14

HESTIA, THE GODDESS OF THE HEARTH

Hestia had fewer temples than any of the other gods of Mount Olympus, but she was worshiped the most of all. This was because she was the hearth-goddess,—that is, the goddess of the fireside,—and so had part in all the worship of the Greek home.

The Greeks said that it was Hestia who first taught men how to build houses. As their houses were so very different from the ones in which we live, perhaps you would like to know something about them. In the days when these old Greeks were so brave and noble, and had such beautiful thoughts about the world, they did not care much what kind of houses they lived in. The weather in their country was so fine that they did not stay in-doors very much. Besides, they cared more about building suitable temples for the gods, and putting up beautiful statues about the city, than they did about building fine houses for themselves.

So their houses were usually very small and plain. They did not have a yard around the houses, but built them close together, as we do in some of our large cities. Instead of having their yard in front, or at the sides of the house, they had it in the middle, with the house built all around it. That is the way many people in other lands build their houses even now; and this inner yard they call a court-yard. Around three sides of the court-yard the Greeks had pleasant porches in wh8ich the boys and girls could play when it was too hot for them to be out in the open yard And opening off on all sides from the porches were the rooms of the house.

In the middle of one of the largest of these rooms, there was always an altar to the goddess Hestia. This was a block of stone on which a fire was always kept burning. The Greeks did not have chimneys to their houses, so they would leave a square hole in the roof just over the altar to let the smoke out. And as they had no stoves, all the food for the family was usually cooked over this fire on the altar.

Whenever there was any change made in the family they offered sacrifices to Hestia. If a baby was born, or if there was a wedding, or if one of the family died, they must sacrifice to Hestia. Also whenever any one set out on a journey, or returned home from one, and even when a new slave was brought into the family, Hestia must be worshiped, or else they were afraid some evil would come upon their home.

The Greeks thought that the people of a city were just a larger family, so they thought that every city, as well as every house, must have an altar to Hestia. In the town-hall, where the men who ruled the city met together, there was an altar to the goddess of the hearth; and on it, too, a fire was always kept burning. These old Greeks were very careful never to let this altar fire go out. If by any chance it did go out, then they were not allowed to start it again from another fire, or even to kindle it by striking a bit of flint and piece of steel together,—for of course they had not matches. They were obliged to kindle it either by rubbing two dry sticks together, or else by means of a burning-glass. Otherwise they thought Hestia would be displeased.

The Greeks were a daring people, and very fond of going to sea, and trading with distant countries Sometimes, indeed, part of the people of a city would decide to leave their old home, and start a new city in some far-off place with which they traded. When such a party started out, they always carried with them some of the sacred fire from the altar of Hestia in the mother city. With this they would light the altar-fire in their new home. In this way the worship of Hestia helped to make the Greeks feel that they were all members of one great family, and prevented those who went away from forgetting the city from which they came.

15

DIONYSUS, THE GOD OF WINE-MAKING

The gods of Mount Olympus did not always remain high up in heaven, out of the reach and sight of men. The Greeks told many stories of what they did on earth as well. You have read that Artemis loved to wander over the mountains, and hunt the deer in the forests. Hephaestus had his workshops wherever there were great volcanoes. Hermes often appeared to men as a messenger from Zeus; and the other gods also would often come down in the shape of men or women to give advice or reproof to their favorites.

But the god Dionysus did much more than this. For many years he lived on earth among men He was the son of Zeus, though he was brought up on earth by forest-spirits. Perhaps it was from these that he learned to love fresh growing plants and climbing vines full of fruit; but however that may be, he became the god of the grape and of wine. When he was grown, he did not join the other gods on Mount Olympus, but set out on a long, long journey, through all the countries of the world, teaching men everywhere how to plant and tend the grapevine, and how to press the juice from the ripe fruit, and make it into wine.

With him, in his journeys, went bands of strange wood-spirits, who danced and made music before him, and waited upon him. Wherever he and his band were well treated, the god was kind and generous to all, and taught many useful things. But sometimes the kings did not want their people to learn the new things which he taught, and then he would punish the selfish rulers very severely.

At one time during his journey, Dionysus was wandering alone upon a sea-beach, when a ship came sailing by near the shore. The men in the ship were pirates; and as soon as they saw the beautiful youth they sent men ashore, who seized him, and carried him aboard the ship. They expected to sell him as a slave in some distant country, for in those days any one who happened to be made a prisoner could be sold into slavery. But the pirates soon discovered that their prisoner was not an ordinary person. When they tried to tie him so that he could not escape, the ropes fell off his hands and feet of their own accord. Then suddenly the masts and sails became covered with climbing vines full of bunches of rich, ripe grapes, and streams of bubbling wine flowed through the ship. This was all very astonishing to the pirates; and when the prisoner changed from a slender young man into a roaring lion, and sprang upon their captain, they became very much frightened. When a great bear also appeared in their midst, they could stand it no longer, and all jumped overboard except one who had wanted to set the prisoner free. As he, too, was about to jump, Dionysus changed back into his own form, and told him to stay and have no fear The god even took pity on the others, and saved them from drowning by changing them into a sort of fish called dolphins.

When Dionysus had finished his long journey he went up to Mount Olympus, and took his place among the other gods. The people of the earth worshiped him in temples, as they did the other gods; but besides this they held great festivals in his honor each year. One of these festivals came in the springtime, when the vines began to grow; and another when the grapes had ripened, and the wine had been made. At these festivals the people had great processions, and men would go about singing and dancing as the wood-spirits had sung and danced before Dionysus on his journey Poets, too, would sing verses to the music of the lyre, and in these they told about the adventures of the god. At length they began to have theaters, and regular performances in them, at these festivals. So Dionysus became not only the god of the grape and of wine, but also of the theater.

16

PAN, THE GOD OF SHEPHERDS

Pan was not one of the great gods of Mount Olympus. He lived upon the earth, and was the god of the fields and forests and wild mountain sides. Therefore the Greeks thought that he was the protector of herdsmen and hunters, who were obliged to wander far away from the cities and settled parts of the country.

Pan was not beautiful, like most of the gods; indeed, he was a very strange looking figure He had legs and hoofs like a goat, and little horns upon his forehead, so that he seemed half man and half animal. He was a noisy fellow, with a great, deep voice which was so terrible that when he shouted the bravest men would run away in fear.

The people were usually afraid of Pan, and dreaded meeting him when they were obliged to pass through lonely parts of the country. But there was no reason for this; for in spite of his strange shape and his noisiness, Pan was a very gentle and good-natured old fellow. He loved music, and was fond of playing upon a kind of pipe which he made out of the reeds that grow by the rivers. The wood-nymphs and wood-spirits would often gather around, and dance to his music when he played.

Pan was worshiped especially by the country people. But there was one city called Athens where he was honored as much as anywhere else in Greece, and this is the way it came about. Athens was once threatened by a great army, which was coming to destroy the city, and kill or make slaves of its people. The Athenians were afraid that they would not be able to defend themselves alone, and so determined to send to another city called Sparta for aid. For this purpose they chose their swiftest runner, whose name was Pheidippides; and he set out, alone and on foot, for Sparta

The way lay through a rough, mountainous country, where the road became only a rocky path, winding over the mountains and down into the valleys. Pheidippides traveled with all speed, running most of the way, and scarcely stopping for rest or food. After two days and two nights, he entered the city of Sparta, and breathlessly begged them for help. But the Spartans received him coldly, and would give him no promise of aid. Then, without waiting for rest, Pheidippides was off again for Athens, to tell the Athenians that they must fight alone; but his heart was heavy as he thought how easily they might be conquered by so great an army.

As he was racing along the way back to Athens,

he suddenly came upon a strange figure standing by the roadside. It was the god Pan, with his smiling eyes, curling beard, and great goat-legs. Pheidippides stood still in fear; but the god called to him kindly and said:—

"Why is it, Pheidippides, that they do not worship me, and ask me for help, at Athens? I have helped them many times before this, and they may be sure that I will help them now."

Then the god disappeared, and Pheidippides' fear was changed to joy. He sprang forward upon the road, running faster than ever to carry the good news. When he reached Athens, the people were comforted by the promise which the god had given him, and they marched bravely out to battle with as large an army as they could gather. Their enemies had ten soldiers for every one that Athens had; but the thought of the god gave them courage, and they fought so well that they won the victory, and the city was saved. Many of the Athenians used to tell afterward how they saw the great god Pan fighting on their side that day, and overthrowing the enemy by hundreds. Perhaps they only imagined it, but at least they believed it very earnestly; and after that battle the Athenians always worshiped and honored Pan more than did any other people in Greece.

17

HELIOS, THE SUN-GOD

The Greeks did not know that the earth was round. They believed that it was flat, and that the sun moved over it each day from east to west. They thought that each morning the goddess of the Dawn threw open the eastern gates of the sky, and the golden chariot of the sun rolled out. This was drawn by twelve swift horses, and was so brilliant that men's eyes could not bear to look at it. In the chariot stood the god Helios, with the rays of the sun flaming around his head.

It took great skill to drive the chariot on hits long day's journey. Helios had to guide it with much are, so as not to drive too near the earth and scorch it. The way during the morning was up a steep ascent. At noon the chariot reached the summit of the course, and began to descend toward the west. The way then was rough, and the descent so steep that the horses were in danger of falling headlong. But

the journey was always finished in safety, and the
weary horses entered the gates of the Evening.

There were two beautiful palaces for Helios, one
in the east at the gates of the Dawn, and the other in
the west at the gates of the Evening. To get from his
western palace back to his palace at the gates of the
Dawn, Helios, with his horses and the chariot of the
sun, was obliged to sail underneath the world
during the night in a golden boat made by the god
Hephaestus.

Helios had a son named Phaethon, who wished
greatly to drive the chariot of the sun, and begged
his father to allow him to guide it for one day. The
god at first refused, saying,—

"Only my hands are strong enough to drive those
spirited horses upon that dangerous road."

But Phaethon would not be denied. He begged
until at last his father consented. Helios placed the
young man in the flaming chariot, and fastened the
burning rays of the sun around his forehead. Then,
as Dawn opened the eastern gates, the horses
sprang forward. Bu they soon felt that their master's
hands were not upon the reins. Phaethon was much
too weak to guide the twelve strong horses. They
dashed from the track downward toward the earth,
setting fire to mountain-tops and forests, and
boiling the water in the rivers and brooks. Then
they whirled up among the stars, burning them, and
setting the very heavens on fire.

When Helios saw what terrible mischief was
being done, he begged Zeus for aid. To save the
world from being destroyed, Zeus hurled a mighty

thunderbolt at Phaethon, which struck him, and knocked him headlong from the sky. Then he sent a great rain, which lasted many days. Finally, when the flames were out, the gods saw how great the damage was. Whole countries were left bare and blackened; and though the plants soon began to grow again almost everywhere, some places are still barren to this day. And some races of men were so scorched by the great heat that the color of their skins has remained black or brown ever since.

18

THE ELDER GODS

The Greeks did not believe that Zeus and the other gods of Mount Olympus were the only ones that had ever ruled over the world. They thought that there had been other great gods long before Zeus, or Poseidon, or Hades, had even been born.

Uranus was the first ruler of the gods, while the earth was still young, and there were yet no men on it to be governed. He had many children, who were called Titans. These were huge, fierce gods, and even their father sometimes found it difficult to control them. Indeed, some of them were so strong and terrible that Uranus did not dare to allow them the freedom of the earth and sky, but kept them shut up tight and fast in the very deepest and darkest places inside the earth. Three of these prisoners were giants, each with a hundred hands; and others of them had only one great eye in the middle of the forehead.

Uranus may have been quite right in dreading these strange gods, and putting them away where they could do no harm; but their mother was angry when she discovered that they had been fastened in the depths of the earth. She was not strong enough herself to set them free, so she could only try to punish Uranus for his cruelty. She gave her youngest son Cronus a sharp sickle for weapon, and told him to drive his father Uranus from the throne of the gods.

Cronus succeeded in wounding Uranus, and took the throne himself; and he and the other Titans ruled together for a long time. But Cronus never felt secure upon his throne; for he was always fearing that one of his own children would overthrow him, as he had overthrown his father. At last this really came to pass. Zeus and Hades and Poseidon were the children of Cronus; and after many years they rose against him, and drove him from the throne.

But although their king was conquered, the other Titans did not give up without a struggle. There were many of them, and they were still very strong and powerful; so they tried to regain what had been conquered by the younger gods. The battle between them lasted for ten long years, and the Titans seemed almost victorious. But at last Zeus set free the hundred-handed and one-eyed giants from their prison in the earth, and asked them to help him. Then they came rushing to his aid, bringing thunder and lightning and earthquakes as weapons. With their help the Titans were conquered, and buried deep under the islands of the sea, so that they might never make further trouble.

Zeus kept the thunder and lightning, which the giants had brought, as his especial weapons, and ruled as king of the younger gods. But he felt as unsafe upon his throne as his father Cronus had felt before him. He was always fearing lest some one of the gods should become stronger than he and conquer him, as he had conquered Cronus, and Cronus had conquered Uranus.

Sometimes the gods were afraid of those who were not gods at all, and who were much less powerful than the Titans whom they had conquered. Perhaps you will remember Otus and Ephialtes, the two young giants who put Ares in a vase, and kept him shut up fro so many months. After they had succeeded so well with Ares they seemed to think that it would be a good plan to treat all the gods in the same way, so that men might be left to themselves upon the earth, with no one to rule over them, or tell them what they should or should not do. So they set about making war upon the gods. As they were mortals, like the other men upon the earth, Otus and Ephialtes could not follow the gods high up in heaven; so to get at them they began to pile one mountain on top of another. When the gods saw the two young giants moving the great mountains of the earth, they were afraid for a while that they might be driven from their homes in the sky. But Apollo, the archer, came down from heaven in a cloud, and soon the two giants were shot dead by the arrows from his golden bow.

19

PROMETHEUS, THE FIRE-GIVER

In the great war between the elder and the younger gods, two of the Titans took sides with Zeus against their brother Titans. The chief of these two was Prometheus; and it was because Zeus followed the wise advice which he gave, that the friends of Cronus were defeated, and Zeus became king of the gods in his place.

We should suppose that after this Zeus would have honored Prometheus always, and treated him as kindly as possible. But instead of that, in a little while Zeus became very angry with him, and punished him more severely, almost, than any one else was ever punished. This is the way it happened.

When Zeus became king of the gods, the men upon the earth were nothing more than savages They lived in caves, and wore skins of wild animals, and ate all their food raw because they did not know how to make fires to cook it. Prometheus felt sorry for them, and wanted to teach them many things; but Zeus would not allow him. At last Prometheus decided that he would help them nevertheless. So he stole some of the fire that the gods kept in heave, and brought it down to men hidden in the hollow stalk of a plant. From that time on, men began to make all kinds of things, which they could not have made without the help of fire; and they improved greatly in their manner of living. As Prometheus had also shut up all sicknesses and sorrows in a great chest in his home, so that men might not be troubled by them, it seemed as if they would soon become as happy as the gods themselves.

When Zeus saw what Prometheus had done he was very angry. To prevent men from becoming too proud and powerful, the gods made a beautiful maiden out of clay, and sent her to the brother of Prometheus, to be his wife. She was very curious about everything around her, and one of the first things that she did was to open the great chest which she found in the house. Then all the troubles, which Prometheus had so carefully shut up, at once flew out; and from that day to this, men have had to suffer for the curiosity of this girl, Pandora.

In order to punish Prometheus, Zeus had him chained fast by his hands and feet to a great lonely mountain, where the hot sun shone down on him day after day, and the rains and the storms beat upon him. But Prometheus was as brave and proud as Zeus was cruel. In spite of all that he suffered, he foretold that by and by there would come another god who would conquer Zeus just as Zeus had conquered his father Cronus When Zeus heard this, he sent Hermes to ask who this new god would be. But Prometheus refused to tell, unless Zeus would set him free. Then Zeus hurled great mountains upon Prometheus, and buried him in the earth far down below the world of the dead After many, many years, he brought him up, and fastened him to his mountain again; and then he sent an eagle to pick and tear at his liver every day, while every night the wound healed afresh. But still Prometheus refused to tell the secret that would save Zeus from losing his throne. So for ten thousand years he suffered in this way.

At last Zeus was compelled to yield, and Prometheus was set free. Then he told the danger that hung over Zeus, and how it could be avoided. And by following the advice that Prometheus gave, Zeus was saved from losing his throne.

Because Prometheus had done so much for the race of men, and had suffered so much in their cause, the Greeks were always very grateful to him. But as he was not one of the great gods who ruled the world, they did not build temples to him or worship him, as they did the gods of Mount Olympus.

20

PROTEUS, THE OLD MAN OF
THE SEA

The other Titan who helped Zeus in the great war of the gods was named Oceanus. He had been one of the old sea-gods; and when Poseidon became the god of the sea, he let Oceanus and all his many children have part under him in ruling the great ocean and the other waters of the earth.

The most interesting of all the children of Oceanus was his son Proteus, whose duty is was to care for Poseidon's sea-calves, as the Greeks called the seals. Every day he led them up on the land, where they lay and slept on the rocks and the warm sea-sands. The Greeks never though of Proteus as being young and beautiful like the gods of Mount Olympus. Instead of that they represented him in their pictures and in their stories as an old, old man, covered with the foam of the ocean, and with seaweed and sea-shells clinging to his beard and his long gray hair.

One of the wonderful things that this old sea-god could do was to change into the shape of anything he wished. Once the shipos of a famous Greek king, while they were sailing back from a great war, were blown about for a long while, so that he could not reach home. The king was told that some god was angry with him, and that the only way to reach home would be to seize the god Proteus, and force him to tell him what to do.

So at daybreak one morning the king and three of the bravest and strongest of his men set out for a cave by the shore, where Proteus came every day. There they made hollows in the sand, and lay down in them, and covered themselves with the skins of some sea-calves that they had brought with them. In a little while great numbers of sea-calves came out of the water, and lay down beside them in the cave and went to sleep. At noon Proteus himself came and counted his flock, and then he, too, lay down to sleep in their midst.

Then the king and his men sprang up, and seized the old sea-god. To escape from them, Proteus tried all his changes. First he became a great lion with a shaggy mane Then he became a panther. Then he changed to a snake, and twisted and turned in their hands. Then he became a tree, covered with rustling leaves. Then he changed into flaming fire; and last of all he turned into flowing water.

But in spite of all these wonderful changes, the

king and his three brave men held fast to the god. Then Proteus saw that he was beaten. So he changed back to his own form, and told the king all that he wished to know. After this the king got safely home at last.

21

EROS, THE LOVE-GOD

The Greeks told many wonderful stories about Eros, the love-god, some of which are very hard to understand. Long before Zeus, or Cronus, or Uranus, was the king of the gods,—indeed, before these gods were born, and before there were any plants or animals,—Eros was a god as powerful as he was in the later days when the Greeks wrote their stories about him.

They said that in the beginning the whole world was all one mass of stone, and there was no earth or sky or sea. Then Eros, or Love, was the only living thing; and just as the mother-hen warms her eggs till the little chicks peep out, so the Greeks said Love brooded over the world until living things appeared, and the world began to take shape.

Although he was so very, very old, the Greeks thought that Eros always remained a youth, never growing up as the other gods did. And they represented him in their pictures as a beautiful lad, with a golden bow and a quiver full of arrows. Some of his arrows were sharp and of the whitest silver. Whoever was wounded with one of these at once began to love the person that Eros wished him to love. Others were blunt and made of lead; and if a person was struck with one of these, he did just the opposite, and disliked whomsoever Eros wished.

One of the stories which the Greeks liked to tell about Eros was of his love for a young girl, and the way in which she became immortal through it. This girl's name was Psyche, which means "the should;"

and she was so beautiful that as soon as Eros saw her he fell deeply in love with her.

She was only a mortal, however, while he was a god; so when they were married he could not take her to Mount Olympus with him, nor even let her know who he was. For many months they lived together very happily in a beautiful palace of marble and gold, though Psyche was never allowed to see her husband by daylight nor to light a lamp by night.

Indeed, Psyche was so happy that her sisters began to be jealous of her good fortune, and said that her husband must be some dreadful monster, who was afraid to let her look upon his face. Psyche did not believe this, of course; but, in order to prove that they were mistaken, she did something that took away her happiness for a long time.

After Eros had fallen asleep one night, she lighted a lamp, and brought it to the bedside When she saw that her husband was the god Eros, she was so startled that a drop of hot oil fell from her lamp upon his face, and he awoke. Then he saw that she had disobeyed him; and, after giving her one sad look, he was gone.

Poor Psyche was heart-broken, for she knew that he would not come back again. She wandered about for a long time, going from temple to temple, trying to find some way to make up for her fault and regain her husband. At last she came to the temple of Aphrodite, where she was given a number of hard and dangerous things to do.

First she was shown a great heap of beans, barley, wheat, and other grains, all mixed together, and told that she must sort out the different kinds before the sun set At once thousands of ants came to help her, so that before evening the task was done. The next day she was sent to a distant grove to get a lock of wool from a flock of fierce, golden-colored sheep that fed there. When she came to the river by the grove, a reed whispered to her that when the sun went down the sheep lost their fierceness, and then she would find bits of the wool caught in the bushes all around; and so she finished this task successfully. Last of all, she was sent down into the dark underworld to get some of Persephone's beauty for Aphrodite. This, too, she was able to do, by following the wise directions which the winds whispered to her, and with the help that Eros gave to her unseen.

Having finished all her tasks, Psyche was forgiven her fault, and was then made immortal by the gods so that she might never die; and ever after that she lived happily with Eros in the beautiful home of the gods on Mount Olympus.

STORIES OF THE HEROES

1

HERACLES

Heracles was not one of the immortal gods, like Hermes or Pan. He was the son of a Greek king, and only became immortal because of his great deeds while living upon the earth. From his babyhood Heracles was much stronger and braver than his comrades, and as he grew to be a youth he became the wonder of his father's city He was not always thoughtful, however, in the use of his great power over others; and sometimes he used all the strength of his powerful body without thinking at all what would be the result.

As Heracles was a prince, he was taught all there was to be learned in those days. He had masters for all his studies, and even had a music teacher who was to teach him to play upon the lyre. One day, as the teacher was giving Heracles his lesson, he was obliged to correct him for mistakes that he had made. This made Heracles very angry, and without thinking what he was doing he struck his teacher with the instrument upon which he had been playing.

His blow was so sudden and fierce that the man fell dead, and then Heracles wished that he had not grown so strong. Of course his father, the king, was very angry at what he had done. He said, that , as Heracles could not control his temper and keep from harming other people, he had no longer any right to be a prince. So he sent him away from his palace to a lonely mountain to be a shepherd there.

Heracles did not like this tame and quiet life, where he had only the sheep for companions After trying it for a while, he went to the oracle at Delphi to ask if there was not some other way in which he could make up for his thoughtless deed. The oracle showed him such a way; but it was so difficult to that no one would even think of trying it, unless he was very strong and very brave. This was to perform twelve of the hardest tasks that could be imagined. Heracles was so sure of his strength and courage that he began them with a light heart, and thought that he would soon accomplish all that was asked of him. But he found these labors much more difficult than he had thought they would be, and it was twelve long years before the last was done.

As his first task, Heracles was asked to kill a fierce lion that lived on a lonely mountain and was a terror to all the country round about. He did this without a weapon of any kind, by hunting it to its den, and then strangling it in his arms. He took the skin from this lion, and wore it around him as a garment, and cut a great club, which he carried in his hand. So you will see him in almost all of the pictures and statues that were made of him.

The next task of Heracles was to kill a great water-snake called the hydra. This snake had ten heads, one of which was immortal; and he found that this task was not so simple a thing as crushing the lion to death in his arms. As he cut off each head, two more immediately grew where the one had been, and he was worse off than before But he finally discovered a way to destroy the snake by burning off the heads instead of cutting them, and at last he was ready to begin his third task.

This was not to kill a dreadful beast, but to do something much more difficult. He was to bring a wild boar alive from the place where it lived in the depths of the forest to a certain city. He succeeded in doing this as he had done the first two tasks; and he walked into the town dragging the great beast behind him, to the terror of all the people. The king was so frightened that he rushed away, and hid in an underground hut in the forest. It was only when Heracles had turned the animal loose, and it had disappeared from the city, that he came back. And then he ordered Heracles to be very careful not to bring any more proofs of his bravery into the town, but thereafter to show them outside the city walls.

His fourth task was to capture a deer belonging to Artemis, and bring it also home alive. This deer had horns of gold and hoofs of brass, and was the swiftest animal of its kind. Heracles followed it for a whole year over plain, mountain, and valley, through winter and summer. Each time he neared it, it would bound away, and he could never quite catch it. At last he wounded it with an arrow, and so caught it, and carried it on his shoulders to his city.

Heracles continued to do successfully all that was asked of him. One of his tasks was to drive away and destroy great birds which fed on human flesh, and which could shoot out their feathers like arrows at those who came near them. Another was to get a girdle which the god Ares had given to the Queen of the Amazons. Another was to cleanse in a day a filthy stable where three thousand cattle were kept; this he did by turned a river through it, and letting it wash the filth away. Another was to capture a mad bull which belonged to Poseidon. And another was to bind and bring home from a distant country a herd of fierce horses which fed on human flesh.

But the most wonderful of all his labors were the two which he performed last. These were to find and carry home the apples of the Hesperides, and to bring the three-headed dog Cerberus up from the under-world. Heracles had no idea where to find the apples of the Hesperides, and went up and down the world asking where he should go for them. At last one of the sea-gods told him that he must look for them on some islands far to the west. So he traveled toward the setting sun until he came to where the god Atlas stood holding the blue heavens above the earth upon his shoulders Here Heracles found that he could go no farther, so he persuaded Atlas to go get the apples for him while he held the heavens in his absence.

Atlas readily agreed, and slipped his heavy burden upon the shoulders of Heracles. Atlas obtained the apples; but he enjoyed the freedom from his burden so much, that, when he came back with them, he proposed to take the apples the remainder of the way home, and leave Heracles to do his work for him. But Heracles had no idea of allowing this. He did not wish to spend the rest of his days standing still under a great burden while Atlas roamed free and happy about the world. So he pretended that he was willing that Atlas should do as he wished, but asked, as a favor, that Atlas would hold the heavens for him a moment while he fitted a cushion to his back, so that he might support the burden more comfortably. Then, when Atlas had kindly taken the burden again, he snatched the apples and hurried away.

The last labor of Heracles was the most terrible one. He was sent to the under-world, where gloomy

Hades reigned, to get the dog Cerberus. The journey was so difficult that Hermes and Athena were obliged to go with him and guard him on the way. Hades gave him permission to take the dog if he could do it without club or weapon; and Heracles seized him in his arms, and carried him so to the upper world. This deed was so wonderful that he might never have done anything more all his life long, and still have been the greatest of all heroes. But as long as he lived he continued to wander over the earth and meet with great adventures. When he died at last, he was so beloved by the gods that he was taken to Mount Olympus and made immortal, instead of being sent to the dark under-ground world of the dead.

2

THESEUS

Theseus was the son of King Aegeus of Athens, who ruled over the city in very ancient times But although Theseus was the son of the king, he was not brought up at Athens He lived with his mother and grandfather far from his father's country, and grew to be a lad of sixteen before he even knew that he was a king's son. When he reached that age he was a strong and handsome boy. His mother looked upon him proudly and yet sadly, for she knew that the time had come when he must leave her.

One day she led him to a great stone, and told him a story that left him breathless with excitement. "Under this stone," she said, "are hidden a sword and a pair of sandals, placed there long ago by your father. When you are strong enough to lift the stone, you are to place the sword at your side, and strap the sandals on your feet, and go to Athens to claim the place of prince of the city. Will you try to lift the stone now?"

Without a word, Theseus put his shoulder to the rock, and using all his strength he rolled it from its place. Then he snatched the sword and sandals which he found in the hollow beneath the stone, and prepared to set out upon his journey to his father's kingdom. In those long-ago days a journey by land was very dangerous because of the robbers and wild beasts that might attack the traveler; besides, Theseus was still only a lad; so his mother and grandfather urged him to go to Athens by sea. But Theseus would not listen to this. He wished to take the hardest road, and prove himself to be really as brave as he felt that he was. So he set out by land, and before he reached Athens he had almost as many adventures as Heracles

One of these adventures was with a robber called Procrustes. This man did not kill the people whom he captured in any ordinary way, as by shooting them to death with arrows or cutting off their heads. He had a bed upon which he laid his prisoners; and if they were not just the right length for it, he would either cut them off or stretch them out until they should exactly fit it. When Theseus heard of him, he at once set out to punish him. With his great strength he easily captured him; and then he treated him as Procrustes had so often treated others, and let him find out for himself how it felt to lie upon his bed.

After many adventures with wicked men and fierce wild beasts, Theseus at last reached Athens.

His father, King Aegeus, did not know that he was on the way; and it was so long since he had hidden the sword and sandals under the rock for his son, that he had almost forgotten it. He had grown to be a sad and lonely man, who was afraid that even his best friends and nearest relatives were trying to get his kingdom from him. He had been told by the oracle at Delphi to beware of the many who should come before him with but one sandal. HE was always looking for this man; and when one day Theseus came to his palace wearing only one sandal, having lost the other on the way, he felt at once that he had found his worst enemy.

He gave a feast that very night, to which Theseus was asked to come; and he made ready a cup of poison which he meant to have him drink. But, before the cup was offered to Theseus, the meat was passed at the table. Now, in those days they did not have table-knives as we do. Each guest was expected to use whatever he had with him in the way of a knife. When the turn of Theseus came to cut his piece from the meat, he drew his father's sword, which he had brought carefully through all of his adventures on the way. King Aegeus saw it and recognized it, and knew in an instant that this young man must be his son. The cup of poison was thrown away; and, even though Theseus had come to his father with but one sandal, he was welcomed, and made price of the city.

He had not been long in Athens when he found something to do more difficult than anything he had met with on the journey. Not far from the city there was an island where a cruel king named Minos lived. This king had once crossed the sea to Greece, and burned the town of Athens. Before he left the Athenians in peace, he made them promise to send an offering to his island every nine years of seven youths and seven maidens. These prisoners Minos fed to a monster called the Minotaur, which lived in a cave that had so many windings and turnings in its passageways that a stranger who had once gone in could never find the way out again.

Soon after Theseus came, the offering to Minos was prepared. The boys and girls were to be chosen by lot from among the noblest families in the city, and every father and mother was in fear lest their son or daughter might be chosen. All the people were angry at King Aegeus for allowing such a thing to be done; and they were whispering among themselves that they ought to choose a stronger and braver king, who would be able to protect their city, and not send their children to a dreadful death. Then Theseus came among them and offered of his own free will to go with the youths and maidens. King Aegeus objected to this, and begged his son not to leave him; but Theseus was determined to seek out the Minotaur and kill him. So when the vessel left the town, with its black sails and its burden of weeping young men and women, the Prince Theseus was upon it.

King Aegeus was very sorrowful as he saw his strong young son leave him. He had not much faith that Theseus would succeed in killing the Minotaur. But, before the vessel left, he had given to the captain a white sail, and ordered him to hoist that instead of the black sail as he returned to the city, if Theseus had been successful and had killed the monster. But if he had not succeeded, the captain was to raise the black sail, and then all the people would know as soon as they saw the ship that their children would return to them no more.

When Theseus arrived at the island of Minos he found unexpected help to aid him in his fight with the Minotaur. The king's daughter took pity on him, and gave him a thread to guide him out again through the winding passages. Holding this in his hand, he went bravely in, and killed the monster with his father's sword. Then, still holding fast to his slender thread, he found his way out as he had come in, and set sail joyfully for Greece.

But he and his companions were too excited over their happy escape from King Minos and his Minotaur to think of changing their sail from black to white, as King Aegeus had told them to do. So they came in sight of Athens with the funeral sails under which they had started. The king was watching for them from a high cliff; and when he saw the black sails of the vessel, he was sure that his son had failed and would never return again. In his grief and despair he threw himself from the top of the steep hill and was killed.

Thus Theseus by his thoughtlessness did his father the greatest harm, and the people all said that the Delphic oracle had spoken truly when it told King Aegeus to beware of the man who came before him with but one sandal. But the Athenians did not grieve long for King Aegeus. They were too glad to receive their children back, and to learn that the Minotaur was at last dead. They made Theseus their king in his father's place, and under his long rule Athens became a great and powerful city.

PERSEUS

Perseus freeing Andromeda

There was once a king in Greece who did a very cruel thing. An oracle had foretold to him that he would be killed by his own grandson. He was determined that this should not come to pass, so he tried to cheat the gods. He placed his beautiful daughter and her baby son in a chest, and threw them into the sea, thinking that by doing this he would never see them again, and need never fear his little grandson.

But the waves were kind to the princess and her child. The chest floated lightly upon the water, and at last came to rest upon the sandy beach of an island. Here it was found by a fisherman, and the princess and her child were received and cared for by the ruler of the island. They lived there for many years, while the boy, who was called Perseus, grew to be a strong and active youth. For some time the people were very kind to them; but at last the ruler of the island became vexed at the mother of Perseus, and made her his slave. Then, because Perseus had become such a strong young man, the king began to be afraid that he would try to avenge the injury which had been done to his other. So he sent him far away on a dangerous journey, to the very ends of the earth.

There dwelt a terrible woman called Medusa, the Gorgon. The hair of the Gorgon was a mass of living snakes; and she was so hideous to behold, that just to look upon her turned one to stone. Perseus was commanded to bring home the head of this woman; and although he set out obediently, he did not know at all where to find her. But while he was wandering helplessly about, the god Hermes and the goddess Athena came to his aid, and gave him courage for his dreadful task. They told him that he must have a pair of winged sandals to help him on his way, and also a helmet which would make him invisible.

These wonderful things were in the cave of some water-nymphs, and he could find out where these nymphs were only by going to some dreadful old woman who had but one eye and one tooth among them. These they were obliged to pass around from one to the other as they needed them. Hermes led Perseus to these old women, and then left him. At first Perseus could not get them to tell him what he wished to learn. But when he stole their one eye as they passed it from one to another to look at him, they were glad enough to tell him what he wanted, in order to get back their eye again.

When at last Perseus reached the cave of the nymphs, he easily obtained the sandals and the helmet. Putting these on, he soon reached the cave of Medusa, and found her lying asleep on the ground. But he did not dare to approach her face to face, for fear lest he should be turned to stone. Then it was that the goddess Athena came to his aid, and gave him her bright shield to use as a mirror. Holding this before him, Perseus walked backward, looking not upon Medusa, but only upon her reflection in the shield. When he was near enough, he struck off her head with a curved sickle which Hermes had given him, and, still without looking at it he thrust the head into a bag, and hurried away.

As he journeyed back from the ends of the earth toward his home, many adventures befell him, and he found that the Gorgon's head was a wonderful weapon. It was better than a sword or a spear; for, if he wished to harm his enemies, he had only to take Medusa's head from its bag, and hold it before their eyes; then at once they were turned to stone.

One of his adventures ended in his gaining a beautiful princess as his wife. As he passed through the country of the Ethiopians, he found every one in great distress. The queen of the country was a very vain woman, who had boasted that she was more beautiful than the nymphs who lived in the sea near by. This had made the nymphs so angry that they had begged the great god Poseidon to punish the queen. He did this by rolling a great flood of his salty water upon the land, and sending with it a sea monster, that devoured both beasts and men. The country suffered so much from these misfortunes that the king sent to an oracle, to discover how they might escape from t hem. The oracle replied that the only help was to sacrifice the king's daughter Andromeda to the sea monster.

For a long time the king refused to do this; for Andromeda was a beautiful girl, and he loved her dearly. But at last he could resist the wishes of his suffering people no longer. Andromeda was led from her father's house to a rock upon the seashore, and chained there alone, to await the coming of the monster. But, before she had been harmed, Perseus passed that way. He wondered at finding a beautiful maiden weeping in chains, and went to her aid. He killed the monster as it came out of the deep, and broke the chains that found Andromeda. Then they went together to her father's city; and Perseus claimed Andromeda as his bride, because he had saved her from a dreadful death.

The people were glad enough to be rid of the monster, and to have their beautiful princess back alive one more; but they did not wish to give her away again to this strange young man. So Perseus took her without their consent; and when some of them tried to prevent it he turned the men to stone with his Gorgon head, and went on his way homeward with Andromeda at his side. When he came to his old home, he used Medusa's head again. This time it was the man who had mistreated his mother whom he turned to stone. In his place as king he put the good fisherman who had found him and his mother in the chest on the shore of the sea.

Then Perseus went across the sea to find the grandfather who had been so afraid of him when he was a little child. When the old king learned that his grandson had not been drowned after all, and that he was alive and coming to see him, he was more afraid than ever. Now he was sure that the oracle would come true, and that this young man would kill him for what he had done so long ago to him and his mother So he fled from his city, and hid himself. But Perseus followed him and found him, and showed him that he came only to do honor to him. Then his grandfather welcomed him, and ceased to fear him, and caused games to be held to celebrate the coming of this strong and noble grandson who had come to him in his old age. But, alas! In the midst of the games a dreadful accident happened. One of the games was hurling the quoits;

and as Perseus was throwing the round, flat piece of iron, it slipped from his grasp, and struck his grandfather so that he fell dead. So the oracle was fulfilled at last.

Perseus was so sorry for what he had done, that he would not accept the throne of his grandfather, though the people wished him to do so. He exchanged this kingdom for another one, where he would not always be reminded of what he had accidentally done; and there he lived happily with Andromeda for many years.

JASON AND THE QUEST OF THE GOLDEN FLEECE

While Heracles and Theseus were doing the wonderful deeds of which you have read, a band of heroes under the leadership of a prince named Jason went on a voyage which brought them adventures that were just as remarkable. This was the quest of the Golden Fleece. You must first know what this Golden Fleece was, and how Jason came to go in search of it.

There was once a boy and a girl whose stepmother was very cruel to them, and wished to put them to death. But the god Hermes sent them a winged ram, whose fleece was of pure gold; and seating themselves on this they flew far away from their cruel stepmother. Over mountains and plains and valleys the ram bore them safely; but when they were passing over an arm of the sea, the girl, Helle, became so frightened that she lost her hold, and was drowned. The water into which she fell was ever after called the Hellespont, or the sea of Helle.

The boy clung fast to the ram, and at last was brought safely to a far-off country, where his step-mother could not find him. There he sacrificed the ram on the altar of Zeus, and its beautiful golden fleece was hung up in a grove that was sacred to the god Ares. To keep it quite safe from any one who might try to steal it, a terrible dragon was set to watch it night and day.

By right, Jason was king of one of the lands of Greece; but his uncle had taken the throne from him, and said he would not give it up unless Jason should bring him the Golden Fleece. Jason was a brave, adventurous young man, and he agreed to do this. So he had a great ship built, with fifty long oars to it; and this ship was called the Argo, from the name of its builder. Then Jason sent word of his plan throughout Greece, and soon he had forty-nine of the bravest men in Greece to go with him. And because the ship was named the Argo, people called the band of men who went in it upon this long journey the Argonauts, or the men who sailed in the Argo.

Getting aboard of their long ship, they set out; and for many days with sail and oar they journeyed on, going ever to the east and north. Passing through the Hellespont, they came to another narrow strait. There the way was blocked by two great moving rocks which clashed together and ground to pieces the ships that sought to pass through the strait. Here the Argonauts waited many days before they could find a way to get their ship through.

At last a wise man of the neighborhood told them to watch the flight of a dove as it went between the rocks. They did this; and when they saw that the dove had only her tail feathers caught and pulled out, they determined to venture on the passage. They chose the time when the wind was strongest to fill the sails, and all the heroes pulled their hardest at the oars. The Argo slipped through the crashing rocks just in time, and only a few ornaments at the stern of the vessel were broken off

When they had passed this danger the Argonauts soon reached the country of the Golden Fleece. There Jason went to the king, and told him of his journey with his band of heroes, and asked him for the fleece. The king was a cunning man; and although he had no idea of giving this stranger the beautiful fleece, he said that Jason could have what he wanted if he would do two tasks for him. This Jason promised to do; but when he heard what these tasks were, his heart sank within him, for they were very difficult. But Medea, the king's daughter, came to his aid, and with the help of her enchantments he was able to perform them both.

The first task was to harness two mighty bulls, whose hoofs were of solid brass, and whose breath was scorching fire, and with this team to plow a field that had never been cultivated. Medea gave him a magic salve to rub over his body, which protected him from the fiery breath of the bulls, and gave him strength to yoke and drive them. So this task was accomplished in safety.

The second task seemed still more difficult. This was to sow in the furrows he had made the teeth of a dragon, and to kill the armed men who would then spring out of the ground Jason could never have conquered such an army of warriors, so he was forced to find some trick to help him. Here, again, Medea aided him.

"When the armed men spring up," she said, "throw a large stone among them, and they will fall to fighting one another." Jason did this; and the warriors, instead of attacking him, turned upon one another, and fought until they were all killed.

When the king learned how Jason had accomplished his tasks, he was very angry both at him and at Medea; and he refused to give up the Golden Fleece. So Jason would have failed, after all, if it had not been for Medea's help once more. That very night they went together to the grove of Ares, where the fleece was kept There Medea put the dragon to sleep with her enchantments; and then Jason took the fleece and hastened away to the Argo. The ship was all ready to go to sea; and Jason set sail immediately, taking Medea with him.

The journey towards home was not so dangerous as the outward trip had been, and at last Jason came happily into his own country again. When he gave the Golden Fleece to his uncle, however, he did not get his kingdom again in return, as his uncle had promised him. The king had never supposed that he would see Jason again; and now when he came back, and brought the Golden Fleece with him, he was not ready to keep to his bargain. But Jason and Medea were determined to have the kingdom; and, as usual, it was the enchantress Medea who found the way. By a trick she got the kingdom for Jason, and then they became king and queen.

Jason and Medea did not rule long nor happily. Perhaps they had been too cunning and too tricky to be happy in the end. It was not long before a son of Jason's uncle came, and drove Jason from the throne, so that he was forced to flee from the country. And at last, after much sorrow, he was killed by the falling of a rotten beam upon him in the old ship Argo.

5

ACHILLES AND THE WAR ABOUT TROY

If you were to go aboard a ship in Greece, and sail toward the east, you would before many days come to the mainland of Asia. There, in another country and another continent from Greece, was in olden times a famous city called Troy. Here lived a strong, brave race of people, who had made their city great by their industry in peace and their courage in war.

The king of this people was a good man named Priam, who was much beloved by every one. He had many children, so many, in fact, that one more or less did not matter much in his great household. But one day another little son was born to King Priam, and the priest said that he would grow to be a danger and a trouble to his family and his country. To prevent this trouble, King Priam had his servants take the baby, and leave it on a barren mountain-side to die. There some shepherds found the child, and reared him carefully; and he grew to be a tall, beautiful youth, very active and skillful in all sorts of games.

When Paris—for that was the boy's name,—had become a young man, he was called upon to decide a very odd question. Among the gods there was one who was called the goddess of Discord, because she was always causing quarrels wherever she went The other gods did not like her, so they did not invite her to a great feast to which the other gods were all asked. Then the goddess of Discord took a beautiful golden apple, and wrote on it, "To the fairest," and tossed it among the other gods as they feasted. At once a quarrel arose as to who should have the apple. Of the three great goddesses,—Hera, Athena, and Aphrodite,—each claimed that she was the fairest, and that the apple was for her. As none of them would give up, they had to ask some one to decide which one was the most beautiful.

Now, none of the gods wished to decide the question for fear lest he should offend the goddesses. So it was agreed to leave the decision to one of the children of men; and Paris was the judge whom Zeus chose. When the goddesses heard who was to be the judge, they each made haste to bribe him to decide in her favor. Hera, as queen of the gods, promised him power. Athena offered to make him the wisest man in the world; and Aphrodite promised him the most beautiful woman for his wife Paris chose the latter gift, and gave the golden apple to Aphrodite.

Not long after this, King Priam held games at

Troy, in which the young men of the kingdom were invited to try their strength with one another. The shepherd lad Paris joined in all of these games, and was so skillful that he was the winner of the prize. Then a priestess revealed that he was the son of Priam; and in spite of the trouble that had been foretold form this son, Priam received him gladly, and restored him to his place as prince of Troy.

It was not long, however, that Paris was content to remain in Troy. He wished to see the world, and find the beautiful wife whom Aphrodite had promised him; so he sailed away across the sea to Greece. There he came to the court of a king named Menelaus, whose wife, Helen, was the most beautiful woman in all that land. As soon as he saw Helen, Paris knew that her was the wife that Aphrodite had intended for him; so he stole her away from her husband, and carried her back with him to Troy.

This led to a great war between the Greeks and the Trojans. King Menelaus, and his brother, King Agamemnon, called upon all the kings of Greece to join them in trying to get Helen back, and in punishing the Trojans. After many months the fleet that was to carry them across the sea was ready, and a great army set sail. When they reached troy they left their ships, and camped upon the plains around the walls of the city. The Trojans closed their city gates, only coming out now and then to fight the Greeks. For many years the war dragged on. It seemed as if the Greeks could not take the city, and the Trojans could not drive away the Greeks.

In this great war, even the gods took part.

Aphrodite, of course, took the side of Troy, because it was through the promise she had made to Paris that the war had begun Hera and Athena both took the side of the Greeks. Of the other gods, some took one side and some the other; and long after this the Greeks loved to tell how men sometimes fought even against the gods.

Agamemnon was the leader of the Greeks, but the bravest man and the best fighter was Achilles This prince was the son of a goddess of the ocean and of a Greek king, and possessed wonderful strength and beauty. When he was a baby, his goddess mother had dipped him in the waters of a dark river in the kingdom of Hades, and he had become proof against any weapon except at one little place in the heel, where his mother's hand had prevented the water from touching him. When Agamemnon and Menelaus called upon the men of Greece to fight again Troy, Achilles gladly took his shield and spear and joined them, although it had been foretold that he should meet his death before Troy. There he fought bravely; and even Hector, the eldest son of King Priam, and that champion of the Trojans, did not dare to stay outside the walls while Achilles was in the field.

In the tenth year of the war Achilles became very angry at a wrong that had been done him by Agamemnon. After that he refused to join in the fighting, and sat and sulked in his tent. When the Trojans saw that Achilles was no longer in the field, they took courage again. Hector and the other Trojan warriors came forth and killed many Greek heroes, and soon the Greek army was in full flight. The Trojans even succeeded in burning some of the Greek ships.

Then the Greeks were very much dismayed, and sent to Achilles, and asked him to help them. But he was still angry, and he refused. At last the dearest friend of Achilles came, and begged him to aid them once more. Still Achilles refused; and all that he would promise was to let his friend take his armor and go in his place. So his friend took the armor of Achilles and went forth, thinking that the sight of Achilles' arms would once more set the Trojans flying. But soon word was brought to Achilles that Hector had slain his friend, and carried off his armor

Then Achilles saw that his foolish anger had cost him the life of his friend. His grief was very great; and he threw himself upon the ground and wept, until messengers came to tell him that the Trojans were carrying off the body of his friend, so that the Greeks might not bury it. Achilles sprang to his feet, and rushing toward the battlefield without chariot or armor he shouted in wrath. The goddess Athena joined her voice to his; and the sound startled the Trojans so that they turned and fled, leaving the body of Achilles' friend in the hands of the Greeks

The next day Achilles put on a new suit of armor which his goddess mother had obtained from the god Hephaestus, and rushed into battle again to avenge his friend. All day long the battle raged about the walls of Troy, the gods fighting among men to protect and aid their favorites. At last at the end of the day, when the Trojans had been driven back within their walls, Hector alone remained without. After a fierce battle Achilles slew him; and so great was the anger of Achilles, that he tied the feet of the dead Hector to his chariot, and dragged him through the dust to the Greek camp.

But Achilles himself did not live much longer. As he was fighting one day soon after this, and arrow shot by Paris struck him in the heel,—the one spot where he could be wounded,—and he was killed.

After Achilles was dead the Greeks could not hope to take Troy by open fighting, so they tried a trick. They pretended that they were tired of the long war, and that they were going home. They built a wooden horse as tall as a house; and leaving that in their camp as an offering to their gods, the Greeks got on board their ships and sailed away. Then the Trojans came flocking out of their city to examine this curious thing which the Greeks had left behind. Some of the wiser heads feared the wooden horse, and wanted to burn it; but the others said that they would take it into the city, and keep it as a memorial of their victory over the Greeks.

So they took it within the city walls. That night after the Trojans were all asleep, a door opened in the side of the wooden horse, and a man slipped out. Then there came another, and then another, until about fifty of the bravest Greeks had appeared These Greeks slew the guards and opened the gates. The Greeks who had sailed away that morning had come back as soon as night fell, and were waiting outside As soon as the gates were opened they rushed into the sleeping city, and after that night there were only heaps of ruins where the city of Troy once stood.

In the fight of that night King Priam and his queen and all of his children and most of his people were killed. King Menelaus found Helen, and took her back again to his own country. The priest's saying at the birth of Paris had come true He had brought destruction on his family and on his kingdom, and it was right that he also should lose his life in the fall of Troy.

6

THE WANDERINGS OF ODYSSEUS

After the Trojan War was ended by the burning of Troy, the Greeks filled their ships with precious things which they had gathered, and set sail for home. It was not a long journey back to Greece, and some of the princes returned quickly and happily to their own land. But one prince, named Odysseus, had more adventures on the journey back than he had met with before the city of Troy itself; and it was not until ten long years had passed that he succeeded in reaching his native land again

Odysseus had been one of the wisest and bravest men in the battles about Troy, and he proved himself wise and brave in his long and perilous journey home. It would be too much to tell of all the adventures that he had, though some time you may read them in a book composed by a great Greek poet named Homer. Here we can tell only a few of the wonderful things that happened to him.

After sailing for a long time, and seeing many strange lands, Odysseus and his men came to the land of the Cyclops. These were a wild and lawless race of giants, each of whom had only one great eye in the middle of his forehead. They neither planted nor plowed the fields, but lived off their herds of sheep and cattle. Odysseus landed here, and went with some of his men to explore the country. Soon they found a great high cave, with much cheese and milk in it. They entered this to wait till the owner should come; and by and by he appeared, driving his herds into the cave with him.

When Odysseus and his men saw how large and fierce he was, they would gladly have run away; but the giant had rolled a huge rock against the mouth of the cave so they could not get out. When the Cyclops saw them, he immediately showed them what they might expect from him, by seizing two of the men and eating them. The next morning he at two more of them, and then drove his flocks out to pasture. But before he left he rolled the rock back before the mouth of the cave, so that Odysseus and his men were still kept prisoners.

While he was gone, Odysseus planned a way of escape. He found a long stake in the cave; and the end of this he sharpened into a point, and then hardened it in the fire When the giant had come back, and had again eaten two of the men, Odysseus gave him some wine which they had brought with them when they came to the cave. When he had taken this, and was sleeping drunkenly, Odysseus and his men plunged the sharp stick into his one eye and blinded him.

The Cyclops could not see them now, and so he could no longer catch them. The next morning Odysseus and his men got out of the cave by clinging to the under side of the sheep as the giant let them out to pasture. And though the giant felt the *back* of each sheep as it went out, to see that none of his prisoners got away, they all escaped safely. But it happened that this cruel giant was the son of Poseidon, the god of the sea; and from this time Odysseus and his companions had to endure the wrath of the sea-god for what they had done to his son.

After leaving the land of the Cyclops, Odysseus came to the island of Aelous, the god of the winds, who entertained them kindly for a whole month. When Odysseus took leave of him, Aeolus gave him a strong sheepskin bag, closely fastened with silver This held all the winds of heaven except the west wind, which was left out to blow him gently home. With this Odysseus sailed for nine days steadily onward, until he was so near his native land that he saw the people on the shore. Then, while he slept, his men secretly opened the bag of the winds to see what great present it was that King Aeolus had given to their leader. All the winds of heaven leapt from the bag; and storms raged about their heads, and blew them out across the sea, until they reached the very island of King Aeolus from which they had departed After that King Aeolus refused to help them.

Next Odysseus came to the island of an enchantress named Circe. Here some of his men were changed into swine by her. But by his bravery and the help of the god Hermes, Odysseus overcame the enchantress, and forced her to change them back into men again. Then Odysseus and his companions lived pleasantly with her for a whole year; and when at last they were ready to set sail again, Circe told Odysseus what he must do to get safely back home. This was to go down to the world of the dead, and ask concerning his journey. He did this, and there he was told of the wrath of Poseidon because of what he had done to his son. But he was told also that he should reach his home in spite of Poseidon, if he and his men would only leave untouched the oxen of the sun when they should come to them.

Then Odysseus returned to the upper world, and once more he and his men set out on their way. Again they met with many adventures. At last they came to the island where the oxen of the sun fed in the fields. Odysseus did not wish to land here, but his men insisted on spending the night on shore. When Odysseus had made his men promise not to harm the oxen of the sun, he agreed to this, and they landed. That night a great storm came, and for a whole month they could not leave the place. Their good gave out, and though they hunted and fished they could not get enough to eat. At last, while Odysseus slept, his men killed some of the oxen of the sun and at them; and Helios, the sun-god, was angered at them.

When the storm ceased they set sail again. But

they had not gone far before Zeus hurled a great thunderbolt at their ship because they had eaten the oxen of the sun. The ship was wrecked, and all the men were drowned except Odysseus. For ten days he swam in the sea supported by the mast of his ship. Then he was thrown on the shore of an island which was ruled by the goddess Calypso. Odysseus was kindly received by the goddess, and he stayed here seven years. But he longed to return to his wife and to his native land. At last the goddess agreed to let him go; and on a strongly built raft he set sail once more—this time alone. For seventeen days he sailed on in safety. But Poseidon had not forgotten his old anger against Odysseus. He sent a great storm which wrecked his raft; but Odysseus once more swam shore and was saved.

This time Odysseus found the daughter of the king of the land washing linen with her maidens in a river which flowed into the sea. When he told her his story, she took him to her father; and at last Odysseus was taken to his own home in one of the ships which belonged to this king.

So, after much suffering and many wanderings, Odysseus reached home. But his troubled were not yet ended, for he found that in his absence evil men had taken possession of his property. With the help of his son and a faithful servant, Odysseus succeeded in overcoming them, and got possession of his house and lands. And at last he lived quietly and peacefully once more in the island kingdom over which he had ruled before he set out for the war against Troy twenty years before.

The stories of the gods, and of the Argonauts, and of the warriors who fought around Troy, are what we call "myths." They tell about things which occurred so very long ago that nobody can tell just when they happened, or how much of the story is true and how much is only what the Greeks imagined about it. Now you are to read about things most of which we are quite sure did happen, and which took place just about at the time and place and in the way that the story says. These we call "history," to distinguish them from the myths.

STORIES FROM GREEK HISTORY

1

____

WHAT LYCURGUS DID FOR SPARTA

There were two cities in Greece named Athens and Sparta. These cities were not nearly so large as New York and Chicago; but still they were great towns, because the people who lived in them were brave and intelligent men and women, and did many noble deeds. In each of these cities the people obeyed laws which they said had been established for them by a great lawgiver. In Sparta the lawgiver was named Lycurgus, while in Athens it was Solon who had made their laws. We will read first about these two men and the laws which they made.

When the Spartans came into the land where they built their city they had a great many wars with the people round about them. Once it happened that their king was a boy, and could not defend them; so everything fell into confusion, and the people suffered much from their enemies. Then they called upon the king's uncle, Lycurgus, to help them out of their trouble.

Now, Lycurgus saw that while it would be very easy to drive off their enemies once, the only way to cure the troubles so that they would not come back any more was by making the Spartans better soldiers. So he drew up a set of laws which would do this. Then he called the people together, and explained the laws to them, and asked,—

"Will you agree to do what these laws command?"

"Yes," shouted the Spartans, "we will."

Lycurgus made them promise that they would not change any of the laws until he came back from Delphi, where he was going to consult the oracle. Then he went to Delphi, and the oracle told him that Sparta would be free and happy as long as the people obeyed his laws. When Lycurgus heard this he determined never to go back home again; for he knew that the Spartans would obey the laws as long as he stayed away, but he was afraid that if he went back some of the people might want to change them. So all the rest of hi life was spent far from the land he loved, and at last he died among strangers.

It was wise to Lycurgus not to return to Sparta, for the laws which he had made were very severe. When a boy reached the age of seven years he was taken from his parents, and placed with the other boys of his age in a great public training house. There he lived until became a man. The life which the boys led was very hard. Summer and winter they had to go barefooted, with only a thin shirt, or tunic, for clothing At night they slept on beds of rushes which they themselves had gathered from the river-bed near by. They had to do all the cooking and other work for themselves; and the food which was given them was never as much as hungry, growing boys needed, so they were forced to hunt and fish to get food. They did not study books as you do; but they were taught running, wrestling, boxing, and the use of the spear and sword.

When the boys became men, they left the training-house, and were formed into soldier companies. But still they had to live together, eating at the same table and sleeping in the same building; and it was not until they had become old men, and could no longer serve in war, that they were allowed to leave their companies and have homes of their own. Thus the men of Sparta became strong in body, strict in their habits, and skillful in the use of weapons, and were able to conquer all their old enemies, and to make their city one of the most famous in the world.

But, you may ask, what did the girls do while the boys were put through this severe training? The girls were not taken away from their mothers as the boys were; but they, too, were trained in running, wrestling, and other sports, and so they became the strongest and most beautiful women in all Greece. Although they were not able to fight, they were just as brave as the men, and they encouraged their brothers and sons in their wars. One brave Spartan mother had eight fine sons, who were all killed in one terrible battle. When the news brought to her she shed no tears, but only said: "It is well. I bore them to die for Sparta, if there was need." Was she not as brave as the men who fought the battle?

2

WHAT SOLON DID FOR ATHENS

At Athens the troubles which led the people to call upon Solon to make laws for them did not come from wars with their enemies, but from quarrels in the city itself. There had once been kings at Athens who ruled over the people, but these had been overthrown, and the city was now what we call a republic; that is, certain men were chosen each year to rule over the others. But instead of letting all the people choose these men, as we do in our own republic, only the nobles were allowed to vote. This the common people did not like, so there were quarrels between them and the nobles. Besides this, there was another trouble. Owing to wars and bad harvests, the poorer people in the state had been obliged to borrow money of the rich, and when they could not pay it back the law allowed them to be seized, and sold as slaves. So there was much ill-feeling between the different classes, and it seemed for a time as if they would fall to fighting about these things.

To prevent this, both sides agreed that a wise man named Solon should be chosen ruler for the year, and that he should be allowed to make any changes in the laws that he thought were needed. The nobles thought that Solon would decide in their favor because he was himself a noble; and the people thought he would decide in their favor because he had always shown himself friendly to them.

But Solon did not give either side all that it wanted. First he decided that the Athenians should not be sold as slaves when they could not pay their debts. That was something for the common people. Then he decided that the people who owed money and could not pay it should be helped to do so. This also was a gain for the poorer people; but as they had hoped that they should not have to pay anything at all, they were disappointed. Then he decided that the nobles must let the common people share in the rule of the city. "I gave the people," he said, "as much power as they ought to have without cheating them any, or giving them more than was their share." But this satisfied neither party; as the nobles had expected to keep all the power for themselves, while the people also had hoped to get it all for themselves.

So both parties were dissatisfied with what Solon had done, and the quarrels continued. But after these had lasted for some time, and the Athenians had suffered much on account of them, they at last came to see that Solon was right, and they did as he wished them to do. The laws which Solon had made were cut in great blocks of wood, that they might not be forgotten; and for hundreds of years afterwards these blocks might be seen at Athens.

Many people expected that Solon would not lay down his power when his year was out, and that he would make himself "tyrant" or king. But Solon was too honest to do anything of the kind. When his year was over he went away from Athens, and spent many years traveling. According to a story which the Greeks loved to tell, Solon came once to the court of a great king named Croesus. There the king showed him chests full of gold and silver and many other precious things which belonged to him. Then Croesus asked Solon who was the happiest man in the world, thinking, of course, that Solon would say that he was, because he had so much of what every one wishes to posses. But Solon named a poor man who had died while fighting for his country. Croesus then asked who was the next happiest; and Solon named two youths who had died while showing great honor to their mother. Then Croesus was angry.

"And do you not consider me happy?" he asked, pointing to all his wealth.

"I count no man happy until he is dead," answered Solon.

Many years after this, great misfortunes came on King Croesus. His kingdom was conquered by the king of the Persians, his jewels were taken from him, and he himself was placed on a great pile of wood to be burned alive. Then the words of Solon came to his mind, and he exclaimed,—

"O, Solon! O Solon! O Solon!"

When the king of the Persians heard this, he sent to ask Croesus who this Solon was that he called upon. Then Croesus told him what Solon had said to him, and added,—

"Now I see only too well that Solon was right."

Then the other king had pity on Croesus, and set him free. And the fame of Solon spread so far that he came to be looked upon as one of the seven wisest men of Greece.

3

HOW THE ATHENIANS FOUGHT
THE PERSIANS

After the Persians had conquered King Croesus they began to look across the water toward the Greeks, and to think about conquering them. But it was not until Solon had been dead many years that they tried to carry out their plan. Even then they might not have done so if the Athenians had not made the Persian King very angry by something which they did. Some of the king's subjects were rebelling against him, and the Athenians sent help to them; and in the war which followed the Athenians burnt one of the king's cities. When the king heard this he asked,—

"Who are these Athenians?" for he had never heard of them before.

Then when he was told who they were, he called for his bow, and placing an arrow on the string, he shot it high up into the air and prayed,—

"Grant me, O Zeus, that I may revenge myself on

the Athenians!" And ever after that, as long as the king lived, he had a servant stand behind him at dinner-time and say three times,—

"Master, remember the Athenians!"

When the king's army was ready, he sent them on board ships, and they sailed across the sea to destroy Athens and to conquer all Greece. There were more than a hundred thousand men in the army; and when the Athenians heard that so many enemies were coming they were very much frightened, for they did not have nearly so large an army. They sent the swift runner, Pheidippides, to Sparta, to ask the Spartans to help them. But the Spartans sent back word that they could not come until the moon had reached the full; for their laws forbade them to send out an army until then, and they dared not break their laws.

When the Athenians heard this they were very much disturbed; for the Persians had now landed on their shores, and were only a few miles from their city. But still they marched out their army to meet them; and as they marched, a thousand soldiers came and joined them from a little town near Athens to which the Athenians had been friends.

Even then the Persians had ten times as many men as the Athenians had. So some of the Athenian generals wanted to go back, and some wanted to go forward; and when they voted on it they found that the generals were just evenly divided. Then one of the generals named Miltiades made a speech to the others, and he spoke so well that they decided to do as he wished, and to fight; and all the other generals when their time came to command gave up their turn to Miltiades.

So Miltiades commanded the Athenian army. And when he thought that the time had come to fight, he led his men out of their camp, and charged down upon the Persians. The battle took place in a narrow plain called Marathon, between the mountains and the sea The Persians were so crowded together that they could not use all their men. The Greeks fought, too, as they never had fought before; for they knew that they were fighting for their homes and for their wives and little children, who would be sold as slaves if their husbands and fathers were beaten. So it was not long before the Persians, in spite of their many men, began to give way; and then they began to break ranks, and soon they were running as fast as they could to their ships, with the Athenians following them.

It was a glorious victory for the Athenians, and the Persians were so discouraged that when they got on their ships again they turned about and sailed away for Persia. And that was the end of the first attempt of the Persians to conquer the Greeks.

4

HOW KING XERXES MARCHED AGAINST THE GREEKS

You can imagine how angry the Persian king was when he heard that the Athenians had beaten his fine army at Marathon, and you may be sure that he did not intend to give up trying to punish them. But before he was ready to send another army against them, some of the countries that he had already conquered rebelled against him. So he had to put off his march until he had punished the rebels. Then when that had been done, and before he could get ready for the war against the Greeks, the old king died.

The new king of the Persians was called Xerxes, and he was not nearly so good a soldier as his father had been. Nevertheless, he decided to go on with the war against the Greeks. He was a very vain and foolish man, and wanted the army which he was going to lead to be the largest army that the world had ever seen. So he sent into all the countries over

130

which he ruled, and ordered them to send as many men as they could.

Then men came from all parts of Asia at his command,—black men, white men, and brown men; some clothes in the skins of foxes, leopards, and lions, and others in flowing robes, glittering with gold and jewels; some armed with brass helmets, large shields, long spears, and daggers; others with helmets of wood, small shields, and bows and arrows; and some with nothing for weapons but long sticks, with the ends sharpened and hardened in the fire. Nobody knows how many men there were in this army; but there must have been more than a million, and it may be that there were as many as five million of them.

The army was so great that Xerxes could not get together enough ships to carry it over to Greece; so most of his men had to go by land. At a place called the Hellespont, only a narrow strait separates Europe from Asia; and here it was that Xerxes decided to cross. But to cross he must have a bridge; and thousands of slaves were set to work building bridges made of boats fastened together. Just as these were finished, a storm came up and dashed them to pieces. Then Xerxes was very angry. He sent for the chief builders of the bridges, and had them put to death. And to show how angry he was with the Hellespont, he commanded his slaves to throw chains into the strait, and to beat the water with poles, and to say,—

"This thy master does to thee because thou hast wronged him without a cause; and indeed

King Xerxes *will* cross thee, whether thou wilt or not."

Then King Xerxes had the bridges rebuilt, and when all was ready the great army began to move. And though there were two bridges, and the marching continued without stopping, seven days and seven nights passed before the last man had crossed.

5

HOW THE SPARTANS FOUGHT AT THERMOPYLAE

When the Greeks heard that King Xerxes was marching against them with so large an army, they were greatly frightened. Some of them made peace with the king, and sent earth and water to him, as he bade them, to show that they gave up their land to him. But the Athenians and the Spartans said that they would die before they would give up their land, and become the great king's slaves.

In the northern part of Greece there was a narrow pass, called the pass of Thermopylae, where the mountains came down almost to the sea, leaving only a narrow road between Through this pass the king's army must go to reach Athens and Sparta; and since it was so narrow, the Greeks thought that by sending men to guard it, they might stop the king's army, and so save their country.

It was decided that while the Athenians, who

were the best sailors in Greece, should fight the king's ships on the sea, the Spartans should fight the king's army at Thermopylae. But just at that time there was a great festival among the Spartans in honor of the god Apollo; and although King Xerxes was already marching against their land, they did not wish to slight the worship of their god. The result was that they sent to Thermopylae only three hundred Spartans, under their leader, Leonidas, telling him that they would send more when the festival was over With these three hundred men and a few hundred more that he got elsewhere, Leonidas had to face the hundreds of thousands that Xerxes had, for the other Spartans did not come until after the battle was over.

When Xerxes came in sight of the pass he found the Spartans amusing themselves with gymnastic exercises, and combing their long hair. When he sent to them, and ordered them to give up their arms, they sent back word for him to "come and take them" One of the Spartans was told that the number of the Persians was so great that when they shot their arrows into the air they hid the sun like a cloud "So much the better," he said, "for then we shall fight in the shade."

After waiting four days for the Spartans to surrender, King Xerxes at last sent some of his men to make prisoners of them, and bring them to him. But this they could not do. All that day and all the next day the king's army fought against the Spartans; and though some of the Spartans and many of the Persians were killed, the Spartans would not let the king go through the pass.

At the end of the second day, however, a Greek traitor told King Xerxes of a path which led over the mountain and around the pass.

By this he would be able to send some men behind the Greeks, and attack them from both sides. This he decided to do. On the third day the Spartans fought as bravely as they had done before, but soon the Persians who had been sent over the mountains came in sight behind them. Then Leonidas knew that the end had come. He sent away the men who were not Spartans. But he and his men fought on, for it was considered a disgrace for a Spartan to surrender; and it was only after the last Spartan in the pass was killed that King Xerxes could lead his army safely through.

After the war was over, the Greeks placed a marble lion, in honor of King Leonidas, on the little mound where the Spartans had made their last fight. Near by another monument was set up in honor of his followers, and on it these words were cut:—

> *"Go, stranger, and to the Spartans tell*
> *That here, obeying their commands, we*
> *   fell."*

HOW THEMISTOCLES SAVED GREECE

From Thermopylae, King Xerxes and his army marched down into Greece, punishing the people of all the places that had refused to send him earth and water. At Athens the people were in great fear. They knew that their turn would come next, and that the great king would punish them more severely than any of the other Greeks because they had once burned one of his cities. They sent to the oracle at Delphi and asked,—

"O Apollo! How may we save Athens from the wrath of Xerxes?" But the priestess only answered,—

"Fly to the ends of the earth; for nothing can now save your city. Yet when all is lost, a wooden wall shall shelter the Athenians."

This saying puzzled the Athenians very much. It was some comfort to know that though their city was to be destroyed, they were to be saved. But where was the "wooden wall" that Apollo said should shelter them? Some thought it meant one thing, and some thought it meant another. At last a quick-witted Athenian, named Themistocles, said, —

"The wooden wall means our ships. If we leave our city and fight the Persians on the water we shall win the battle. That is what Apollo promises us. Will you do it?"

Themistocles spoke so well that at last the people agreed to do what he advised. When Xerxes came, they went on board their ships and left the city to the Persians. Then the king pulled down the walls, and burned the city and all the houses in it, as a punishment for what the Athenians had done to the Persian city when his father was king.

When he had burned Athens, Xerxes wished to go on to Sparta and punish it also. The only way to reach that city was by marching along a narrow isthmus which joined the northern part of Greece to the southern; and this he could not do until he had driven away the Greek ships which were near it. These ships were in a narrow strait between an island called Salamis and the shore. They had only one-third as many ships as the Persians had; so when they saw the Persian ships row up to the end of the strait and get ready to fight on the next day, they were very much frightened Only the Athenians were brave and fearless. To keep the other Greek ships from slipping away in the night, and leaving them alone to fight the Persians, Themistocles sent a message to Xerxes, and pretended to be his friend.

"if you want to keep the Greeks from getting away," the messenger told the king, "you must send some of your ships around the island, and shut up the other end of the strait."

This seemed sensible, so Xerxes did as Themistocles advised; and all the Greeks had to stay and fight whether they wanted to or not. The next morning the battle began When the trumpet sounded, the Greeks rowed forward and tried to run into the Persian ships and sink them; and the Persians tried to do the same to the Greek ships. When the ships would come near one another, each side would throw spears or shoot arrows at the other side. Sometimes a ship would get alongside a ship of the enemy; and then soldiers would spring upon the deck of the other boat, and they would fight with swords just as they did on land.

All day long the fight went on. There were two things that were in favor of the Greeks, and which helped to give them the victory. There were so many Persian ships that they were all crowded together in the narrow strait, and could not get out of the way when they saw a Greek ship coming. Besides this, the Greeks were fighting for their homes, while the Persians were fighting only because their king had ordered them to; so the Greeks fought the better. At last, after a great many of the Persian ships had been sunk, the rest turned and fled. The Greeks had won the victory, and Themistocles was the one who had helped them most to gain it.

During all the fight King Xerxes had sat on a golden throne on a hill near the strait. He was very angry when he saw his ships flee, and he had many of his captains put to death. But, as he was a coward at heart, he was a little afraid. Suppose the Greeks should send their brave ships up to the Hellespont, and destroy his bridges of boats, how would he and his army get back to Persia? Besides this, he had punished the Athenians by burning their city; and that, he said, was the chief thing he had come to do. So the great king gave up his plan to conquer Greece, and when the next morning came he was already on his march homeward.

This was not the end of the Persian wars, but it was the beginning of the end. Twice the Persians had seemed just about to conquer Greece, and both times they had failed The first time they had failed because Miltiades had fought so bravely against them at Marathon. The second time it was Themistocles who had prevented them by his skill in bringing about the battle at Salamis. After this the Persians were never again to have the chance to conquer Greece; and when next we shall read about them, we shall see how they themselves were conquered by the Greeks in their own land.

7

ARISTIDES THE JUST

Among the Athenians who fought at Salamis was one named Aristides, who was called "the Just." He is as famous as Themistocles, but for a different reason He was not so quick-witted as Themistocles, nor so good a general; but he was so fair and honest in all that he did, that men said, "There is not in all Athens a man so worthy or so just as he."

Even when they were boys, he and Themistocles could never get along together. Themistocles was a bright lad, but he was so full of tricks and so fond of fun that he was always getting into mischief. Aristides could not approve of this, so he and Themistocles were always disagreeing. When they grew up they took different sides in politics, and continued the disputes which they had begun as boys. Whenever Themistocles would propose anything to the Athenians, Aristides would object to it because, as he said, it was too rash, or because it was not fair to their neighbors, or for some other reason. And Themistocles, too, would object to everything that Aristides proposed.

Now, the Athenians had a law which they had made for just such cases as this. Whenever two leaders could not get along in the city, the law said that the people should meet and decide which of the two should be sent away. Each person was to write a name on a bit of shell, and then the shells were put into a large vase. When all the people had voted, the votes were to be counted, and the man whose name was on the greatest number of shells was to go away and stay for ten years.

This was the law which the people used to settle the troubles between Themistocles and Aristides. While the Athenians were writing the names on the shells, a stupid fellow who could not write came up to Aristides and asked him to write the name "Aristides" on his shell for him. Aristides was surprised at this, and asked,—

"Why, what has Aristides ever done to you that you should want to send him away?"

"Oh! He hasn't done anything," said the man; "in fact, I don't even know him. But I am tired of hearing everybody call him 'the Just' ".

Aristides took the shell without saying another word, and wrote his own name on it. When the shells were counted, it was found that Aristides was the one that had to go

This happened several years before Xerxes marched against Athens. When the Persians came, the Athenians passed a law by which Aristides could return, although the ten years had not yet passed. This Aristides did; and just before the battle of Salamis he went to Themistocles and said,—

"Themistocles, you and I have quarreled with each other for a long time. Let us now cease our quarrel, and only see which of us can do the most good to Athens"

To this Themistocles agreed; and in the battle, while Themistocles commanded the Athenian fleet, Aristides, too, fought bravely against the Persians.

8

HOW PERICLES MADE ATHENS BEAUTIFUL

After the Persians had all been driven out of the land, the Athenians came back to their homes. But now there was only a mass of black and smoking ruins where their fair city had been. The houses were all burned, the walls were only heaps of stones, and even the temples of the gods had been torn down. You can imagine how the women and children felt when they came back from their hiding-places and found the city in ruins. Tears came even to the eyes of the men. But with stout hearts they set to work to clear away the stones and ashes, and before long they had begun the building of a city which was to be larger and fairer than the old one.

But while they were building it they felt they must take care that the Persians did not come back again to tear down what they were rebuilding. So the Athenians and the other Greeks sent ships to keep watch lest the Persians should come again. After a time the other Greeks decided to give the command of this fleet to the Athenians in place of the Spartans, who had always had the lead before. They did this partly because the Athenians had shown themselves to be so brave and wise in the war, but partly, also, because they felt that they could trust Aristides, who was now the Athenian commander. As you can guess, the Spartans did not like this, but they could not help it for a long time.

For many years the Athenians continued to hold the command. During this time their city grew to be rich and powerful, and became the chief city in all Greece. By and by, when Themistocles and Aristides were both dead, a man by the name of Pericles came to have the lead at Athens. He, too, was a great man, but in a way very different from that in which Themistocles and Aristides were great. He was great in his knowledge and love of what was noble and beautiful; and it was to make Athens surpass all other cities in these ways that he set himself to work.

In the midst of Athens there was a high, steep hill with a flat top. In olden times this had been the fort of the Athenians; and before the Persians came there had been a temple to the goddess Athena on it. This has been burned during the war. Now Pericles planned to build in its place not one, but many, temples; and it was on this steep hill that the beautiful buildings sprang up which have made his name famous in all times and in all countries.

Imagine yourself an Athenian boy, and that your father is taking you up this hill to the great festival of the goddess Athena. Only on one side can the hill be climbed, and up this the road winds and turns till it reaches the top. There you come to a gateway or porch of the finest marble, with great tall columns supporting the roof. On the left is a building with rooms filled with pictures and other precious things. Going through the gateway you come out on the top of the hill. Beyond the city you see the blue sea gleaming in the distance. All about you, you see temples and statues. Here is a beautiful temple to the goddess of Victory. Here is a row of statues in honor of heroes, or of Athenian citizens who have won the prize in the games at Olympia. Not far away is a great statue of Athena, the guardian of the city. This statue is taller than the tallest house, and is made out of the swords and shields taken from the Persians at Marathon. From far away at sea the sailors can see the tip of her spear, and then they know that they are nearing home.

Not far from this statue is a temple to Poseidon, the god of the sea. In it is a well of salt water which your father tells you gushed forth there when Poseidon struck the rock with his trident. Coming out of this temple, you walk through a beautiful porch. In this the roof is held up not by columns, but by the statues of six young maidens, clothed in long flowing garments.

But you hurry past these beautiful buildings, so that you may not miss the best part of the festival. You hasten over to the highest part of the hill, and there you come to the largest and most beautiful temple of all. Indeed, it is the most beautiful building that the world has ever seen. It is the temple of Athena, the "maiden goddess." All around it are rows of tall marble columns. Within it is a statue of the goddess, which reaches almost to the roof. This statue is made of ivory and pure gold, and it equaled in beauty and richness only by the statue of Zeus and Olympia. All about the temple are the finest carvings. Here they represent the birth of Athena from the head of father Zeus. There they show the Athenians fighting with the strange creatures, half horse and half man, called centaurs. Here is a long series of carvings showing the great procession of Athenian youths, some on horseback, some on foot, coming to celebrate the festival of Athena And as you gaze at them, longing for the time when you, too, may take part in the worship of the goddess, suddenly you hear your father call,—

"Look, look, my son!"

Then you turn about and look, and there, just coming through the gates and entering upon the top of the hill, you see the procession itself which you have climbed the hill to watch.

9

ALCIBIADES, AND THE WAR BETWEEN ATHENS AND SPARTA

While Pericles was at the head of the government a great war broke out between Athens and Sparta. The Spartans had been jealous of the Athenians ever since the command of the fleet had been taken from them and given to Athens. While Aristides was alive, the Athenians had ruled so justly that the other cities would not help the Spartans against Athens; and as the Spartans did not wish to go to war alone, they had to wait for a better chance.

After Artistides died the chance came, for the Athenians then ceased to rule justly. Many cities besides Sparta began to dislike Athens, because, as they said, the Athenians got money from them to keep up the fleet against the Persians, and then used the money to build fine buildings at Athens. So when Sparta made war on Athens, a great many cities sided with her; and, as many cities still sided with Athens, this became the greatest war that had ever been fought in Greece.

For many years the war dragged on. Children who were born after it had begun were grown men before it came to an end. On the sea the Athenians were victorious everywhere; for they had a strong fleet, and were much better sailors than the Spartans. But on the land the Spartans were the best soldiers; so the Athenians had to shut themselves up in their city, while all the grain in their fields was trampled down and their country houses were burned by the Spartans.

Soon after the war began, Pericles died. Then the government at Athens fell into the hands of men who were not so able as he had been. One of these was Alcibiades, who was a rich young man, belonging to one of the noblest families in Athens. He was almost as quick witted as Themistocles had been; and he might have done as much good to Athens as Themistocles did, if he had wished. But Alcibiades cared only for himself. He was very vain, and loved to strut about in fine purple robes such as only the women wore. He was like a great spoiled child; but the people loved him because he was so handsome and so bright, and because he spent his money so freely.

After Pericles had been dead some time, both sides grew tired of the war, and a peace was made that was to last for fifty years. It really lasted only six years, and it was all owing to Alcibiades that the war began again.

Many miles west of Athens there was a rich city

named Syracuse. This city had taken no part in the war, but Alcibiades thought that it would be a good thing for Athens to conquer it. So he proposed to the people that they send an army to attack Syracuse; and he was such a favorite with them, that the people agreed to do so, and to make him general of the army.

Just before the army sailed away, the people awoke one morning, and found that the images of the god Hermes, which stood before their doors, had been broken in the night This made them very angry. People said that there was only one person that could have committed such a mad prank, and that person was Alcibiades. Alcibiades denied that he had done it; and, indeed, we do not know to this day whether he did it or not. He was allowed to sail away with the army; but his enemies soon persuaded the people to send after him, and order him to return to be tried for the deed.

It was now that Alcibiades showed how selfish he was. He felt abused at what the people had done, so instead of returning to Athens he went to Sparta. There he got the Spartans to begin the war again, and he showed them how they could do most harm to his city. After this the Athenians fared very badly indeed. The army which they had sent to Syracuse was destroyed, and all their ships were lost, and the Spartans became victorious on the sea as well as on the land.

But Alcibiades soon grew tired of the solemn life which he had to live among the Spartans. He felt, too, that the Spartans despised him because he was a traitor. So after a while he sent to the Athenians, and offered to return and help his countrymen against the Spartans. His friends got the people to agree to this; and Alcibiades turned traitor a second time, and joined the Athenians. For a while he was victorious over the Spartans, and it seemed as if Athens would win after all. Then he grew careless, and he lost several battles. At this the Athenians took the command away from him, and gave it to another. A second time Alcibiades left the Athenians; but this time he did not dare go to the Spartans, for fear they would punish him for his treason to them. So for several years he was forced to keep away from the Greeks altogether.

Meanwhile, the long war came to an end. The Spartans conquered Athens, and tore down its walls, so that it would not be powerful any more. Then they turned their attention to Alcibiades, and he was forced to take shelter with the Persians. But even there he could find no rest, and at last he was murdered by some of his enemies. But whether it was by the Spartans, or by some private person whom he had injured, we cannot tell.

10

SOCRATES, THE PHILOSOPHER

Alcibiades Receiving Instruction from Socrates.

It would be hard to find two men who were more unlike than were Alcibiades and Socrates, and yet they were at one time very great friends. Socrates was much older than Alcibiades, but he was the only person for whom Alcibiades seemed to care very much This was partly because Alcibiades saw that Socrates was the wisest man of his time, but it was also partly because Socrates at one time saved the life of Alcibiades

This happened in one of the battles in the long war with Sparta, before Alcibiades had shown what a traitor he could be. The two were fighting side by side in the Athenian army, and both had shown great bravery. Suddenly Alcibiades was wounded, and in a moment more he would have been killed. But Socrates sprang in front of him, and sheltered him with his shield, and so saved his life. At another battle, when the Athenians had been defeated, and were retreating, Alcibiades repaid Socrates. Socrates was on foot, and the enemy was following swiftly after them. Alcibiades, who was on horseback, saw the danger of Socrates, and stayed behind and sheltered him until they reached a place of safety.

But although Socrates fought bravely in the war, he is more famous for the wisdom which he showed in his life, and the unjustness with which he was put to death.

When Socrates was a young man he had a friend who admired him very much, and thought that even then he was the wisest person whom he knew. So once when this friend was at Delphi, he asked the

Oracle if there was anyone wiser than Socrates, and the Oracle answered that there was not. When this friend came home and told Socrates what the oracle had said, Socrates was very much astonished. He was sure that there must be some mistake, for he knew that he was not wise. He was quite sure that the oracle must mean something else.

So Socrates set to work to show that there were other men in Athens who were wiser than he. First he came to one of the men who were governing the city at that time, and who was looked upon as very wise. "If I can only show that he is wiser than I am," said Socrates to himself, "then I can prove that the oracle means something else."

Therefore Socrates asked this man a great many questions. But he found that the man was not wise at all, though he thought that he knew everything. So Socrates came away, saying,—

"At any rate, I am wiser than that man. Neither of us knows anything that is great and good; but he *thinks* that he does, while I *know* that I do not. So I am that much wiser than he is."

Then Socrates went to others who were thought to be wise, and things always turned out in the same manner. He found that the men who were considered to be the wisest were the very ones that knew the least about the things that were the very ones that knew the least about the things that were the most worth knowing about. But whenever he tried to make them see this, they grew angry with him.

Then Socrates saw what the oracle meant by saying that there was no one wiser than he But he grew so interested in his search that he spent all his days in the marketplace, and in other spots where crowds were to be found. And whenever he met with a man who thought that he was wise, he would question him, and ask him what goodness was, and what bravery was, and why some people were good and some were bad; and in this way he would try to show that no one was really wise.

Now, you can readily guess that people did not like this. No one likes to have another person prove to him how little he knows. So Socrates offended many people, and made them dislike him. After this had gone on for some time, the enemies of Socrates determined to try to get rid of him. They brought a charge against him in the court, saying,—

"Socrates offends against the laws by not paying respect to the gods that the city respects, and by bringing in new gods; and also by leading the young men into bad habits."

The last part of this charge was wholly untrue. But the people remembered how badly Alcibiades had turned out, and Socrates' enemies tried to make it appear that this was due to Socrates. Neither was the first part of the charge much nearer the truth. His enemies, however, were ready to believe anything against him; and in spite of all that his friends could do he was found guilty. When the judges called upon him to say what punishment he deserved, Socrates bravely answered,—

"Instead of punishment, O Athenians, I deserve a reward; and if you ask me what it is, I say that I ought to be supported by the State as long as I live, just as those who win in the Olympic games are supported; for I am more worthy of honor than they are."

This saying angered his enemies still more, and they then voted that he be put to death But according to their laws a whole month must pass by before this could be done During this time he lived in prison, where he spent his time talking to his friends, who were allowed to visit him. One day they told him that they had made arrangements for him to escape from the prison and fly to some other city, where he would be safe. But Socrates refused. The laws, he said, condemned him to death; and it was his duty, as a good citizen, to obey them even in that.

At last the day came for his death, and all his friends gathered weeping about him. Socrates took the poisoned cup of hemlock which was given him, calmly and cheerfully, and drank it down as thought it had been water. Then bidding good-by to his friends, he lay down on his couch, and soon he was dead.

There is one saying of Socrates that ought always to be remembered. This is it: "Nothing evil can happen to a good man, either while he is living or after he is dead; nor are the gods unmindful of his affairs."

11

HOW EPAMINONDAS MADE
THEBES FREE

For many years after the close of the war between Sparta and Athens, Sparta was the chief city in all Greece. But once more than Spartans used their power selfishly and unjustly, and so once more they lost their leadership. The city which caused Sparta to lose her high place among the Greeks was one that you have heard nothing about The name of this city was Thebes; and it was about fifty miles from Athens, and much greater distance from Sparta. The people of Thebes were not so bold and warlike as the Spartans; nor could they make such beautiful statues and buildings, or such great poems and speeches, as the Athenians. So the Thebans had never played any important part in Greek history before this. Indeed, the Athenians used to quite look down on them, and call them "dull, heavy, and stupid folk."

Now, at this time Thebes was ruled entirely by

Sparta. There were Spartan governors over the Thebans, and there were Spartan soldiers in the city to make the people obey these governors. Of course the Thebans did not like this, especially as the Spartans had gained this power over them most unjustly. They did not dare to fight openly against the Spartans, because the Spartans were so much better soldiers than they were. So the most daring of the Thebans made a plot to murder the Spartan leaders, and force the Spartan army to leave the city.

One of the Thebans whom the Spartans trusted most invited the leaders of the Spartans to a fine feast at his house. Without suspecting anything, the Spartans came. When they had eaten heartily, and drunk heavily of the wine, their host said that he would next bring in some women to sing and play for them. But the "women" that he brought in were young Theban men, each of whom had a sword his in the folds of his dress.

Just as they entered, a messenger came with a note to one of the Spartans. The Thebans were very much alarmed at this, for they thought that it must be to warn the Spartans of the plot. So it was, but the carelessness of the Spartans saved them from discovery The messenger said that the note was on very important business, and must be read at once; but the person to whom the note was sent, replied,—

"Business can wait until to-morrow." And he thrust the note aside without glancing at it. Thus the Theban youths were able to carry out their plan unhindered, and free their city from its Spartan rulers.

The Theban leaders knew, however, that Sparta would be very angry at what they had done, and that another and larger Spartan army would be sent to punish them. So it was necessary that the Thebans should choose some wise and brave man to be their general in that dangerous time. The man that they chose for this position was Epaminondas, who was one of the greatest men who ever lived in Greece. He had not had anything to do with the plot to kill the Spartan governors, because he was afraid that innocent persons might be killed by mistake. But after the Spartans were driven out, no one did so much for Thebes as Epaminondas did.

In carrying on the war with Sparta, Epaminondas was helped greatly by his friend Pelopidas. The way in which they became such great friends was this. While they were fighting in a former war, Pelopidas was wounded in seven places, and fell so badly hurt that it seemed that he must die. But Epaminondas stepped forward and protected him with his shield, and fought alone with the enemy until the other Thebans could come to his aid. So Epaminondas saved the lie of Pelopidas; and ever after that, as long as they lived, they were the best of friends. There was only one thing that they could not agree about. Pelopidas was rich, while Epaminondas refused to permit, in spite of all that his friend could say.

In this Spartan war the two friends now worked together so well, with so little jealousy or ill-will, that all the Greeks wondered and admired. The two were very different from one another. People sometimes said that Epaminondas was the brain of Thebes, while Pelopidas was her right hand. Pelopidas was a very brave and brilliant soldier; and when he charged at the head of "the Sacred Band" of young Theban soldiers, he would nearly always put the enemy to flight, and win the battle for Thebes. But it was Epaminondas who planned the battles. For the first time he taught the Greeks how to draw their men up in a heavy column which could break even the Spartan line when it charged. So he changed the whole manner of fighting among the Greeks. But he was something more than a great general. He was a great statesman as well,—almost as great as Themistocles had been; and as he was also a very good and just man, you see that we were right in saying that he was one of the greatest men that ever lived in Greece.

For eight years after the Spartans had been driven out of Thebes the Spartan kings kept trying to get that city back again. At the end of that time a great battle was fought between the Spartans and Thebans, which showed how strong the army had become which Epaminondas led. For the first time in the history of Sparta, her army was fairly beaten by a smaller number of men. After that battle—the famous battle of Leuctra—the Spartans gave up trying to capture Thebes; for they now had all they could do to keep the Thebans from capturing Sparta.

Year after year Epaminondas led a Theban army down into the Spartan land. On one of these expeditions his army came even in sight of the city of

Sparta itself, and the Spartan women and children for the first time saw an enemy's camp-fires around their town.

Sparta was a city without a wall, and Epaminondas might now have captured it in spite of all the Spartans could have done. But he did not. Perhaps he thought of the brave stand that the Spartans had made at Thermopylae, and was unwilling to destroy a city that was called "one of the eyes of Greece." At any rate, he turned aside and left the city untouched; though at a later time, when once more he had gotten in sight of the city, he tried hard to take it and failed.

At last the long war drew to a close. First Pelopidas fell, fighting bravely at the head of his troops. Then two years later, in a great battle with the Spartans, Epaminondas was wounded in the side with a spear, and fell dying. When his sorrowing friends gathered around him, he asked first whether his shield was safe. He was told that it was, and that the Spartans had been defeated again. Then he asked for the other generals. Both of these, they told him, had been slain.

"Then," said Epaminondas, "you had better made peace." And having given the best advice he could, he told them to draw out the spear-head from his side. A stream of blood flowed forth, and he breathed his last.

The Thebans followed the dying advice of Epaminondas, and peace was made with Sparta. Thebes never became the leading city in Greece as Athens and Sparta had been, and perhaps

Epaminondas did not wish that it should. But it had broken the Spartan power, and never after the battle of Leuctra was Sparta able to rule any of the other Greek cities in the way that she had ruled Thebes. And the man who more than all others had made this impossible was Epaminondas.

12

KING PHILIP AND DEMOSTHENES

After the power of Sparta had been broken by its wars with Thebes there was no city in Greece which could claim power over the others. They were all free and equal now; and if the Greeks had been as brave and noble and wise as they had been when they fought against the Persians, their cities might have remained free.

But this was not the case. Their leaders now thought more of money than they did of their country, and let themselves be bribed by their country's enemies. And the cities were all so jealous of one another, and each so afraid that some other city might get power over it, that they would not join together to save their freedom So when the king of another country made war upon them, just as the Persian king had done one hundred and fifty years before, the Greeks were beaten, and all their cities lost their freedom.

The people who were to conquer the Greeks were the Macedonians, and their country lay just north of Greece. The Macedonians were not so civilized a people as the Greeks were. They had almost no cities; and most of them lived in the country, herding cattle and tilling the soil. But they were a brave and warlike people, and when they had a strong skillful king to lead them they became very powerful.

While the Greeks were at their weakest the Macedonians found such a king. His name was Philip. While he was still a boy, he was taken as a captive to Thebes, and there he stayed for several years. He was a bright boy, he was taken as a captive to Thebes, and there he stayed for several years. He was a bright boy, so that he learned there all that the Greeks could teach him. The Theban soldiers were at this time the best soldiers in Greece, and from them young Philip learned the art of war. And so well did he learn it, that after he had gone back to Macedonia, and had become king, it was found that he was a better general than any other man of that time.

After Philip had become king of Macedonia, the first thing that he did was to build up a strong army on the plan that he had learned in Thebes. Then he used this army to win some rich gold-mines from a barbarian people who dwelt near his kingdom. After that he had not only a fine army, but also a great treasure to use in carrying on his wars. The next thing that he needed to make his kingdom great was a harbor on the coast, so that ships might come to and go from his kingdom. The Athenians still ruled over several of the coast towns in that region, and by a trick King Philip got one of these. Then he began to plan to go into Greece itself, and make himself master of that country as well.

As you can imagine, the wiser Greeks were very much troubled when they heard how strong this king of Macedonia was becoming. But they were only a few. Most of the Greek cities were so much taken up by their quarrels with their neighbors that they paid little attention to what was going on among the "barbarian Macedonians" And if at any time one of the wiser Greeks thought to warn the others, King Philip would send him such handsome presents and such flattering letters that he would change his mind, and say nothing about the danger. So well did the king succeed in bribing the Greek leaders, that he used to say,—

"No town is too strong to be captured, if once I can get a mule-load of silver passed within its gates."

But there was one Greek that Philip could neither bribe nor flatter. This was Demosthenes, the Athenian. Demosthenes was not a general nor a soldier; indeed, in the only battle in which he took part he became so frightened that he threw down his shield and ran away. But he was one of the greatest orators that the world was ever seen And when it was necessary to tell the Athenians unpleasant things about themselves, and to warn them again King Philip, no man was so brave as Demosthenes.

When Demosthenes was only seven years old, his father died, leaving him an orphan. The guardians who were appointed for him were dishonest men, and they wasted and stole most of the property which his father had left him. So as Demosthenes grew to be a man, he began to plan how he could get the judges to punish his guardians, and make them give up the property which they had stolen.

Now, in those days every man had to be his own lawyer. So Demosthenes began to practice writing speeches and repeating them, so that when the time came he might prove to the judges how unjustly he had been treated. But he had a great many difficulties to overcome. He was awkward and ungraceful in his manner, and his voice was weak, and he did not speak distinctly. To learn to do so, he used to make long speeches with pebbles in his mouth. To make his voice stronger, he would walk along the beach by the sea, and make speeches loud enough to be heard above its roar. And to overcome his awkwardness he used to say his speeches before a large mirror, so that he could see every motion that he made.

At last, after years of practice, he went to law with his guardians, and he made such good speeches that he won his suit. Then he began to take part in politics; and by the time that King Philip had begun to interfere in Greece, Demosthenes had become so great an orator that Philip once said,—

"Demosthenes' speeches do me more harm than all the fleets and armies of the Athenians."

The most famous speeches that Demosthenes every made are those which he made against King Philip. In those orations, Demosthenes told the

Athenians how King Philip was bribing their leaders, and how he was preparing to make himself master of all the Greeks. Demosthenes wanted the Athenians to cease their quarrels with Thebes and other cities, and make war upon Philip. But for a long time the men whom Philip had bribed were able to prevent this, in spite of all that Demosthenes could do

At last one evening as the officers of the city were seated together at supper in the city hall, a messenger came and told them that an army of King Philip had seized a strong place not far from Athens. Now the Athenians saw that Demosthenes was right, and that the danger was real. Everybody ran hither and thither, and all was confusion Demosthenes alone knew what to do. He told them that they must at once send to the Thebans, and get them to help in fighting Philip. This they did; and the Thebans joined them, for their freedom was in danger too.

Then the army of the Thebans and the Athenians marched to oppose King Philip. For several weeks they succeeded in keeping him back. At last one day a terrible battle took place, in which the Greeks fought bravely. But their short spears were of little use against the long pikes with which King Philip had armed his men. So the Greeks were terribly beaten, and after that day they were never free as they had been in the days of Themistocles and Pericles.

13

ALEXANDER THE GREAT

Alexander cuts the Gordian Knot.

When King Philip had conquered the Greeks, he treated them kindly, but he made them choose him to be their leader. Then he told them that he was planning to go on into Asian and conquer the Persians, and the Greeks willingly agreed to help him. But before Philip could carry out his plans he died, and his son Alexander became king in his place.

Alexander soon showed that he was even a greater man than his father had been. While he was still a boy, a beautiful but wild and high spirited horse had been brought to his father's court. None of the king's men could manage it; and King Philip was about to send it away when Alexander said,—

"I could manage that horse better than those men do."

The king heard what his son said, and gave him permission to try it. Alexander ran forward, and took the horse by the bridle. He had noticed that the horse seemed to be afraid of the motion of its own shadow, so he turned him directly toward the sun Then he stroked him gently with his hand until be became quiet.

When this had happened, Alexander gave one quick leap and was on the horse's back, and in a little while he was riding him quietly about the yard. King Philip was so pleased with what Alexander had done that he gave him the horse for his own, and in later years it carried him safely through many battles. Alexander was so fond of it that, at last, when it died, he built it a splendid monument.

Alexander was only twenty years old when he became king, but he soon showed that he could manage his kingdom as well as he could his horses. Because the king was so young, the people that his father had conquered thought that they could now win back their freedom. But Alexander marched swiftly from one end of the kingdom to the other, and everything was soon quiet again. The young king then made ready to carry out his father's plans, and make war on the Persians. Soon he had an army of Macedonians and Greeks ready, and with this he crossed over into Asia

In one of the cities that he came to there was a famous knot, which fastened the yoke to the pole of a chariot. This was the "Gordian knot," and an oracle had foretold that whoever should unfasten that knot should rule over the whole world. Many persons had tried to this, but all had failed. When Alexander came, he looked at the knot for a moment, and then he drew his sword and cut it apart. So he "cut the Gordian knot;" and whether or not it was because of that, he soon did become the ruler of all the world that was then known

Alexander fought three great battles with the Persians; and although the king of the Persians had twenty times as many men as Alexander had, Alexander won all three of the battles This was partly because the Greeks and the Macedonians were so much better soldiers than the Persians; and also it was because the Persian king was such a poor general and such a coward. Almost before the fight had begun, the Persian king would leave his chariot, mount a horse, and gallop away as fast as he could; and of course his soldiers would not fight after their leader had fled.

After the third battle the Persian king was killed by some of his own men, as he was trying to get farther and farther away from Alexander; and then Alexander himself became king of the mighty empire of the Persians. Besides Persia itself, he got Palestine, where the Jews lived then, and Egypt, which was older and richer than any of the other countries. After he had won these countries, Alexander turned and marched far eastward into Asia, looking for other lands to conquer. On and on he marched for many months, over mountains and burning deserts and fertile plains He found many strange lands, and conquered many strange people. But still he urged his army on and on, till they began to fear that they would never see their homes again.

At last they reached India, which you know Columbus had tried to reach by sailing around the world in the other direction. Here Alexander's army refused to go farther; and he was forced, much against his will, to turn about and return to Persia.

But you must not think of Alexander as only a great conqueror. He was a great explorer as well; and wherever he went he gathered specimens of strange plants and animals, and sent them back to learned men in Greece. And as he also sent back accounts of the lands which he conquered, you will see that he added a great deal to what men knew about the world. He was also a wise ruler, and founded many new cities in Asia and in Egypt. After he had returned from India, his mind was full of plans for making one great empire out of the many countries over which he ruled. The capital of this empire was to be in Persia; and the Greeks, the Macedonians, the Jews, the Egyptians, and the people of India were all to have a part in it.

But while he was full of these plans, he suddenly became ill of a fever, and died. He was only thirty-two years old; yet he had been king for nearly thirteen years, and had done more wonderful things than any other king before or since.

Here we must leave the story of the Greeks. After Alexander died, there was no one to rule over his vast empire, and it soon fell to pieces. The Macedonians continued to rule over the Greeks for more than a hundred years longer; then, when they lost their power, there was another people ready to step in, and take their place as rulers of the Greeks. So the old Greeks never got back their freedom; and as a people who are not free cannot have noble thoughts, or do noble deeds, the Greeks never again became as great as they had been in the days of Aristides and Pericles.